To the memory of my mother, father, Auntie Olga and Ah Lan.

Malcolm Jack was brought up and schooled in Hong Kong before returning to university in the UK. As a child, he learned Cantonese at the same time as English. He has had a career both as a public servant and a writer. His writing includes books, articles, reviews on history, literature, philosophy, and politics, as well as travel works on Portugal, and most recently, on South Africa. He is a frequent visitor to Hong Kong.

Malcolm Jack

# MY HONG KONG

AUSTIN MACAULEY PUBLISHERS™

LONDON · CAMBRIDGE · NEW YORK · SHARJAH

A CIP catalogue record for this title is available from the British Library.

ISBN 9781398457133 (Paperback)
ISBN 9781398457140 (Hardback)
ISBN 9781398457157 (ePub e-book)

www.austinmacauley.com

First Published 2022
Austin Macauley Publishers Ltd®
1 Canada Square
Canary Wharf
London
E14 5AA

There are many people to whom I owe a debt of gratitude for having inspired me to write this book. First and foremost, my parents, Ian Jack and Alice Eça da Silva, for bringing me up in an entirely open atmosphere in Hong Kong, so that I was in contact with Chinese culture from earliest days. My amah or nanny, Nina or Ah Lan, as I say in 'First Word', was another mother and she always spoke to me in Cantonese making that an indelible link in my life. There were other important people in those early days, but later were many Hong Kong friends through whom I have continued to share my links with the city. Recently, I have had the benefit of talking to Luka Zhang Lei, Michael Lloyd and Marcia Vale about Austin Coates. Robert Borsje has patiently listened to extracts of the draft and offered useful comments.

The East has all the time, the West has none;
But I know not what I say.
Others must come this way,
To tease the riddle out, if it be one,
Better or not – yet who,
Will find me what I thought I knew?

Edmund Blunden: A Hong Kong House.

# Table of Contents

Preface      11

A First Word, Ah Lan: Malcolm Jack      13

Chapter 1: Myself A Mandarin: Austin Coates      17

Chapter 2: A Many-Splendoured Thing: Han Suyin      32

Chapter 3: Gweilo: Martin Booth      46

Chapter 4: Diamond Hill: Feng Chi-shun      60

Chapter 5: The World of Suzie Wong: Richard Mason      71

Chapter 6: Kampoon Street: Lin Tai-yi      79

Chapter 7: The Monkey King and Sour Sweet: Timothy Mo      88

Chapter 8: The Piano Teacher: Janice Y K Lee      101

Chapter 9: The White Ghost Girls: Alice Greenway      110

Chapter 10: A Change of Flag: Christopher New      116

Chapter 11: Good-Bye Hong Kong: Xu Xi      126

Chapter 12: Fragrant Harbour: John Lanchester      138

Chapter 13: A Chinese Wedding: Simon Elegant      143

Chapter 14: Kowloon Tong: Paul Theroux      148

Chapter 15: Hammer and Tong: David T K Wong      158

Chapter 16: Atlas of An Imaginary City: Dung Kai-Cheung      169

A Last Word Medicine, Music and Archaeology: Solomon Bard      176

Bibliography      181

**Notes**      **184**

**Index**      **191**

# Preface

There is a Tao saying that to travel far is to return. I have travelled the world since my youth in Hong Kong but that early experience, in my formative years, left a mark on me which I have never lost. My roots are there.

In this book I return to the Hong Kong in which I grew up in the 1950s exploring the way a series of writers have seen it, following the story through to the latest, post-colonial period. My aim is to discover what they have made of Hong Kong's mixed identity: was it British, was it Chinese, what else was it? How had it changed? Whose city was it?

The last half century of the colonial period was marked by a series of crises. The shadow of the Communist victory in China in 1949 hung over the city, bringing a flood of refugees from the mainland. While the threat of invasion was always there, it did not dampen the frenzy of economic activity with huge building projects on the Island and in Kowloon. The next crisis came in 1967 when the Cultural Revolution was at its height. Red-guard sympathisers roamed the streets carrying the Little Red Book; there were bomb attacks and attacks on police posts. It again seemed as if Hong Kong's days were numbered. That feeling returned in the 1980s when the negotiations between Britain and China over the exact conditions of the handover due in 1997 dragged on, seemingly without conclusion. Some prominent citizens abandoned ship, not believing that 'one country, two systems' could ever work.

These events form the background and, in some cases, the foreground, of the narratives that I have collected here. They add a tone of excitement and uncertainty to the tales about people at all levels in society over this extended period. The writers I have chosen are a mixed cast: British, Chinese, Eurasian, Korean, American, and finally a Russian Jew; men and women of privileged and less privileged backgrounds. Together they paint a picture of every aspect of Hong Kong from the high life of the colonial elite, ensconced on the Peak to the struggling existence of refugees in the backstreets and squatter camps of

Kowloon. In that way they provide a vivid portrait of every aspect of My Hong Kong throughout this turbulent period.

# A First Word, Ah Lan: Malcolm Jack

Nina exuded good sense and reliability. Her sturdy features, set in a tanned face, her black hair swept back into a bun and sturdy, compact figure presented a reassuringly ordered appearance. Her manner was calm, guided by a practical intelligence which enabled her to cope with anything that came her way. How could any young child not feel safe and comfortable in her hands? Nina, or *Ah Lan* to call her by her Chinese name, was my *amah* or nanny; certainly, the most influential person in my childhood.

Nina's character was the more remarkable given her background. She was from a Chinese Malay family who had come to Hong Kong as refugees. Unable to eke out even a bare living, they abandoned the young girl outside the gates of the Maryknoll Convent where she was found and taken in by the nuns as an orphan. It just happened that mater (as I always called my mum) spent some time as a pupil in the Convent later on, met Nina and was much taken by her. So, when I arrived in swaddling clothes and help was needed, Nina was the obvious recruit to our family home.

Although Nina spoke English tolerably well, we never used it between ourselves. She spoke to me in Cantonese so that Southern Chinese became, in a certain way, my mother tongue. My parents watched this happening without any qualms, knowing that somewhere in my head English was also forming and I understood everything they said to me. But the experience of being 'Ah Mao', the blonde-haired boy who spoke fluent Chinese marked me out for life as a semi-Oriental boy. Of course, it didn't only involve talking. Central to Chinese culture, especially among the gourmet Cantonese, is food. Early each evening Nina interrupted her daily tasks to cook a meal for herself. When she was nearly ready with the food, she would place two wooden stools around her small, low table in the kitchen. Once I was seated on one of them, in a slightly squat position, she would swing over from the stove with at least two savoury dishes – often a fish dish because it was cheaper and a vegetable one, cooked very quickly in the wok. Both were accompanied by a steaming bowl of *bac fan* or white rice. Perched opposite her I used the wooden chopsticks to select tasty morsels from the two metal dishes, then in the local fashion slurped up the warm contents of my bowl. That daily ritual left me with very little appetite for supper with my parents which followed an hour later at the formally laid-out dining table.

So attached had I become to Nina that on her half days off, I kicked up such a fuss that my mother told her that she would have to take me with her on her rounds. Poor Nina – not even a proper day off! Those free afternoons of hers were given over to shopping, with an occasional visit at the time of the C'hing Ming festival to the cemetery to burn false money and light joss sticks in memory of her ancestors lest their neglected spirits came to haunt her. The visits to the cemetery, in the heat of the afternoon, were arduous, clambering up the steep sides of the hill where the graves were placed on platforms cut into the rock. I lurked behind Nina, sucking my melting popsicle as she scrambled up to the point where her own relatives were interred to lay a wreath. If any weeds had grown around the gravestones, they had to be cut out with a small, rounded knife that Nina had brought with her for that purpose. Only on the descent, when everything had been properly done, would she buy herself a Green Spot orangeade from the hawkers who stayed sensibly shaded at the entrance to the cemetery.

The shopping was done in the wonderfully messy Chinese backstreets of Yau Ma Tei in Kowloon where food stalls and hawkers' stands blocked up all the pavements while the traffic streamed by dangerously close to the pedestrians walking on the roadsides. The noise and bustle were immense but nothing was foreign to me – neither the pungent smells from the food stands nor the vulgar, sometimes obscene Cantonese expressions that filled the air. But something was foreign to the locals. '*Wah*! Look at his hair – *gum bak sik*, so white! *Wah*!' Old ladies would advance to try to touch my hair to see if it was real but Nina fended them off with a curt dismissal: "Don't touch his *tow fat*, his hair, it's real, *ghow*, go away."

I wasn't put out by all the attention I got; it amused me and I enjoyed startling the advancing ladies by telling them to shoo off with a blunt, colloquial expression. They stopped and stared at this strange, foreign-devil of a boy who could nevertheless speak to them in their own tongue. One street Nina avoided was one where Sikh dealers hung out, claiming that they were engaging in criminal activities though not specifying what these were, something which naturally raised my curiosity. I wondered why she didn't trust them and whether she was just put out by the strong smell of curry which wafted out of the shop fronts.

On the way home from Kowloon, we crossed the harbour on the Star Ferry, sitting on the lower, second-class deck where foreigners, the *gweilos,* were not usually found. It was crowded with noisy school kids and hawkers carrying baskets of goods. Nina kept an eye out for anyone who came near. 'Not clean, Ah Mao. Don't want anyone touch your hair' she whispered to me as I sat on the bench undoing the crispy wrapper of the sour plum that she had bought for me at the terminal kiosk.

Those halcyon days of wandering in the bustling backstreets came to an end when my schooling started, up on the top of Victoria Peak. The daily trip up the mountain, with the high-rise city cascading below, took on the air of an expedition. Nina would prepare my rattan basket adding a bottle of lemon barley water and some biscuits to the notepad and pencils already in it. Then there would be the inspection – Nina swung me round to make sure there were no marks or creases on my white shirt and shorts which had been crisply ironed. If there were any patches, the clothes had to be changed. The Number 3 bus to the tram terminus in Garden Road was a short ride. Before long we were clambering into the bright green funicular carriage, me in the lead making for the seats at the front, reserved for the Governor, which were unlikely to be taken. Nina followed showing the conductor our tickets, carrying the rattan basket. Soon the tram was ascending the steep track – Kennedy Road, MacDonnell Rd until it lay almost vertical at May Road. I always had an impulse to leap out at that stop, just to test whether one could in fact stand up despite the steep incline that the station was built on. But the stop was brief and, in any case, I was jammed in near the window so could not get past Nina. Not long after that, the tram moved into its parking position at the summit of the Peak and we jumped out. From there we had to walk to school, perched on a hill further along the summit. How interminable that walk seemed to be along the road and up the steep path to the school, especially in the sweltering heat of summer! For an adult it wasn't a long walk but Nina regulated her pace to mine. In the beginning I only attended in the mornings so that Nina waited for me at the school's entrance and we walked back to the tram station together in the blazing midday heat. Lunch would be a bowl of noodle soup in the small shop which was situated just across the road from the station rather than in the more salubrious restaurant next to it. 'Better than shop (she actually meant the restaurant)' Nina would say to me 'cook quick, tasty'. Slurping it up I hardly had time to agree.

Ah Lan was my Chinese mother.

# Chapter 1
# Myself A Mandarin: Austin Coates

In his account of his time in Hong Kong, or more precisely in the New Territories, Austin Coates begins by telling his reader that at the tender age of twenty-six, he was directed by the British Government to serve in Hong Kong as a magistrate and that to do so, he would need a sword. He adds the droll comment:

*Never having had any direct dealings with a government, I found this communication surprising.*[i]

Austin was the son of Eric Coates, the composer of light music and a viola player who performed under the baton of Henry J. Wood, founder of the Proms concerts. Austin says that he was born into a world of music and theatre where everyone, 'regardless of race or tongue, in a sense spoke the same language'. [ii]This cosmopolitan approach was enhanced by his education in France as well as in England. It explains a great deal about his openness to other cultures which is very evident in his attitude to China and the Chinese when he eventually got to Hong Kong.

During the war Austin, like many other bright young things, worked for British Intelligence, in his case with the RAF. In that capacity he visited many parts of the Far East including Burma, Malaysia and Indonesia. His time in the Hong Kong Government Service was from 1949–56 after which he left for Sarawak to take up the post of as Chinese Affairs Officer and later moved to Kuala Lumpur and then Penang. In 1962 he resigned from the Colonial Office to become a full-time writer and returned to Hong Kong as a private resident rather than in an official capacity. He later divided his time between Portugal and

Hong Kong. In Portugal he lived in the bucolic surroundings of Colares, near Sintra, the old royal summer residence.

His most highly seminal book was *Myself A Mandarin* (1968) which is the memoir of his time in Hong Kong as a magistrate. A later novel, *The Road* (1959) is set in Lantau and draws on his experience as a magistrate. In the *City of Broken Promises* (1967), although set in late eighteenth-century Macau, he focuses on the relationship between Chinese and foreigners very relevant to his observations about Hong Kong. For that reason, it was featured in the Hong Kong Arts Festival 1968 in a musical form. As a historian of Macau, he wrote a history of the British involvement there; as a biographer he brought to life the Filipino national hero, José Rizal. Other books on the Western Pacific Islands and Basutoland indicate what we would now call his global range.

Austin joined the Hong Kong Government service at a particularly turbulent time. The backdrop was the war in mainland China between the Communists and the Nationalists with the Communists gaining ground and eventually reaching the border with Hong Kong, presenting a threat to the British Crown Colony. In other parts of Asia there were also insurrections and violence. A large number of refugees – possibly as many as 700,000 – came into Hong Kong from China swelling the population to over 2.3 million. Some of these later returned to the mainland; others stayed bringing considerable entrepreneurial skills and money to the expanding and booming city. Among the refugees were Nationalist soldiers who had escaped capture by the Communists.

In the event the Communists did not invade Hong Kong but the massing of the Red Army on the Chinese side, meant a closed border which had to be manned day and night. On the other hand, the Chinese presence ended some of the pirating that had previously taken place from mainland bases and menaced shipping in the whole area. What Austin found remarkable was the lack of interest among Hong Kong people (the term 'Hong Konger' is of much more recent vintage) in what was going on across that border. Despite the shadow cast from China, the general public in Hong Kong seemed unperturbed. Austin speculates that they had inherited something of the small village mentality that had co-existed with the growth of the Victorian port-city, remaining almost entirely absorbed with local problems. Yet the most pressing of these problems, such as pressure on resources, was the direct consequence of the turmoil in China and the refugee crisis it created for Hong Kong. He observes:

*Never was Hong Kong's separateness from China, and events there, more manifest.* [iii]

Austin took up his duties as the Special Magistrate in the New Territories. The New Territories was largely rural, as he puts it:

*A delightful relic of the Ching dynasty which, avoiding any direct experience of the Revolutions of 1912 and 1949 has come almost unscathed into the world of television and transistor radios.* [iv]

Cases brought before him were settled on principles of Chinese custom and practice rather than on English common law, similar to adaptations found in many British colonial territories. He comments wryly that following Chinese custom and practice was just as well since he knew little about English common law.

The New Territories – ceded to the British for ninety-nine years in 1898 – was very different from the increasingly urbanised areas of adjacent Kowloon. Austin notes that the city/country divide left young men in the rural villages with the feeling they were left out of the progress and prosperity of neighbouring Kowloon. Their exclusion fuelled a sense of inferiority which led some of them to join the Communist party. Being side-lined was a loss of face which dented their pride even more than their poverty. Officials working from central government departments took the view that the industrial and residential expansion of the city was the most important thing happening; to them the village dwellers appeared to be mere yokels whose preoccupations were parochial and against the spirit of progress that pervaded the rest of the colony. Pandering to their customs would be a retrograde policy. In a curious sense, the New Territories was not really Hong Kong and not really China. Much of the area and the islands around had never been administered by any authority other than that of the village elders. The local, patriarchal system remained in place until population growth and urban expansion gradually changed the rural character of great pockets of the area.

The cases that came to the magistrate's court were very much village-level business – problems arising from the continual erosion of rural life as the city expanded; disputes about land and tenancy; parochial and personal tiffs. Austin quotes the administrator-philosopher, Hsun Ch'ing who, in the third century BC, gave a job description of a District Magistrate which still applied in the mid-twentieth-century New Territories. The great sage said:

*The Duty of the local official is to adjust matters between town and country, to harmonise clashing interests (i.e., mark out land etc.): to control the building of houses, to train stock, superintend arboriculture. He should advance morality, encourage filial and fraternal piety, all in their appropriate times – and urge people to obey the government and live quietly and at ease.*[v]

Promoting general peace and harmony was a duty the young magistrate expected but superintending moral standards of the community came as something of a surprise to him. But that was what was expected of him in his role in the New Territories where the traditional Chinese way of settling disputes, which had been in place for thousands of years, was understood and accepted by the local people. Nor was there any written guide he could consult except for an ancient, Jesuit manuscript gathering dust in the university library. For a young man of Austin's age to pose as a figure of wisdom and authority was no mean challenge. His memoir charts his progress in becoming a fair adjudicator; his innate sympathy with the locals and their way of settling things stands out on every page of his account. As his time in office continues, he takes up the mantle of protecting the less favoured rural communities from urban encroachment.

One of the key persons in the magistrate's story is Mr Lo, the court's clerk/interpreter. We are told that he is a very experienced, middle-aged man who is not given to outbursts of expression. But he is an effective guide whose hints that the magistrate is not going along the right path in settling a case are given in slight changes of expression on his face. Austin begins to appreciate Mr Lo's long experience and expertise and wonders whether it would not be better if he were the adjudicator of the cases coming before the court. But he pulls himself together: the British Government service must not be let down.

Mr Lo has to make clear decisions in translating from Chinese to English. When a farmer is asked if his cow grazed on a disputed field, Mr Lo has to decide whether the man's ambiguous answer means a 'Yes'; 'a little' or 'No'. He decides to take the middle path of 'a little'. Although Austin came to form his own views about the cases that came before him, he soon realized that Mr Lo was endowed with a practical wisdom, as well as being very experienced, which was an invaluable boon for the Special Magistrate. He also began to understand that what appeared to be the interpreter's abrupt manner, sometimes almost shouting at the litigants, was a necessary check on proceedings which would otherwise drag on indefinitely.

The first observation Austin makes about the nature of Chinese culture is that it is unfathomable to a foreigner. Whatever appears to be the explanation for any behaviour turns out to be only a scratch on the surface, the inner significance of which is totally different from what a Westerner would expect. Anyone who wants to understand the Chinese way of thinking needs a Mr Lo to guide him. On the other hand, if an outsider showed an interest in wanting to understand the Chinese way of thinking, Chinese friends would be more than helpful, going to great lengths to explain its seemingly tortuous patterns. Outwardly, however, they would show no sign that they were giving advice so as not to cause their foreign friend to lose face. Sometimes silence indicated dissent. When Austin asked friends to admire a pair of portraits of a Manchu official and his wife which he hung at home, his Chinese friends merely nodded and giggled. It was only later that he discovered that those posthumous portraits should only be hung on the annual day of the dead. He had them removed from his walls.

Austin says that one of the difficulties of understanding what the Chinese are thinking is their habit of cloaking their feelings in a facial mask which gives the outward appearance of containment and control: their proverbial inscrutability. That quality has led to a widely held belief by Westerners that the passions and emotions of the Chinese are less strong than those of other human beings. In fact, they are a highly passionate people, something the Special Magistrate discovers as local cases come before him, revealing the intensity of the participants' feelings. Matters are also obscured by the use of euphemisms, more common in Chinese than in any other language. Certain subjects, like sex, were never alluded to directly. Patience and close attention were required so that the underlying motives and objectives of all the parties to any dispute could gradually emerge.

One of the manifestations of the outward control was in the manner that negotiations were conducted. The Chinese approach seemed to the foreigner to be indirect and indefinite. Too much directness led to an avoidance of any issue rather than an engagement with it – the method for reaching a conclusion was to go round the subject, finding out where a convergence of view could take place. If necessary, some details were left unresolved so that they could be decided later when good will had been created between the negotiating parties. When certain etiquette was not observed – for example making sure that the parties involved were properly entertained and of course, well fed – the negotiations tended not to succeed. Austin saw examples of that way of going about business which seemed so roundabout to the Western mind every day in the courtroom. Overriding all other considerations was the need to save face; if necessary, one lied to maintain one's dignity.

Some of the disputes that came before the magistrate involved different Chinese groups. They could be about personal, matrimonial matters as well as property claims. One such case involved a clash between a Hoklo speaking man – a man from a wandering tribe of estuary fisherman (who, like the inhabitants of Aberdeen on the south side of Hong Kong Island passed their lives entirely on boats) and his common law wife. The first difficulty was to find an interpreter to facilitate the use of a third language (after Cantonese and English) in the court. The traditional Chinese way of communicating, through the written language, could not be used since the parties were illiterate. In the end the dispute between husband and wife seeking an annulment of their marriage was reluctantly agreed to by the Magistrate. He could see in the expression of the woman before him that no compromise was going to be possible. Not only would he have preferred reconciliation between the man and the woman but he signed the document granting the couple a divorce in the knowledge that, in fact, they had never been legally married in the first place.

One question Austin considers is whether the Chinese mindset was in any way changing in the sense of disregarding traditional beliefs and practices, particularly in the frantic post-war boom which encouraged a relentless pursuit of wealth. He observed that while young people outwardly might laugh out at the idea of *feng shui*, they nevertheless tended to take steps to prevent any misfortune that would disturb the peace and harmony of their homes by making sure that the rooms faced the right direction. That involved checking on the direction of the wind as had always been carried out prior to deciding the way a room should face and so on. In other traditional areas of practice, the younger generation showed the same tendency not to depart from accepted norms of behaviour. Worship of ancestors was one of the most important rituals in Chinese culture. Then, as now, foreigners could not help but notice how young people attended with their family elders at the tombs of their predecessors to pay their respects. There was no sign of that ritual diminishing.

Austin sees the link between the Chinese obsession with death and the professed Buddhism of its people to be to a superficial. The Buddhist cloak has been a useful cover up in answer to constant probing by Westerners about what religion the Chinese practice. Even though the Chinese have a deep concern with the spiritual world of their ancestors, they do not share the pessimism inherent in the Buddhist idea that all worldly things are imperfect. The Cantonese, in particular, enjoy life to the full, especially when it comes to food. Nevertheless, when a death occurs in the family, at some expense to themselves, they will hire Buddhist priests to chant prayers of appeasement for the departed soul. That does not prevent them from lampooning Buddhist monks on the stage or taking a negative attitude to women who spend too much time in prayer.

Another subject Austin is keen to explore is the Chinese attitude to foreigners:

*But, in China, who are your friends? Your friends are those who have come to know and esteem you sufficiently to enable them to forgive, but not overlook, the fact that you are a foreigner. They are those who are aware that you are genuinely trying to behave properly, according to Chinese canons, and who, though they will be embarrassed, are prepared to forgive you when you unintentionally say or do something indelicate or indiscreet.*[vi]

Whilst many things change in China, they do so within the pattern of Chinese culture. The sense of innate superiority over all foreigners is something that does not change.

One or two anecdotes from the Magistrate's bench are highly amusing. As one case dragged into the lunch hour, proceedings were interrupted by the appearance of a boy from a well-known noodle shop with the Special Magistrate's lunch. The deliverer breezed in without hesitation, put the tray in front of Austin and then, with a sweeping gesture, took the lid off the dish. A cloud of steam arose and the succulent odour of the 'incomparable noodles' filled the air. There was nothing for it – the noodles had to be eaten. The Magistrate continued to hear the case while munching his lunch, claiming that the reactions of the various parties watching him revealed a great deal about their respective characters and helped him to reach a judicious decision. Moreover, he records that the noodles were delicious.

On another occasion, exasperated by the intransigence of parties before him, Austin pulls out a cigar, noticing Mr Lo looking at him cautiously. He asks, *sotto voce*:

*Is it considered proper to smoke while hearing cases, Mr. Lo?*
*Most district officers find it a help, sir.*
*Good, can you ask someone to find me a match?*
*The necessary orders were issued.*[vii]

Sometimes the Special Magistrate had to admit defeat. In one case, a landlord who had probably resorted to bribery, managed to get a permit to build a wall right through an area of small shops with the obvious intention of getting rid of the smallholders. The smallholders petitioned the Magistrate to try to stop the process. However, the permit was granted by a government official in the central office despite Austin's attempt to stop the greedy landlord so as to protect the smallholders. There was nothing more he could do. In a touching sequel to the episode, the shopkeepers presented him with an ivory seal, inscribed with his name in Chinese characters as thanks for taking up their cause even though he had failed to prevent the landlord's scheme. Austin is left speechless when the gift is brought to him by a smiling, young man who disappears before he can be thanked.

When a demand was made that a matter be settled according to English common law, Austin became flustered as he knew his own command of its principles was weak. Moreover, he took the view that because proceedings became more formal with oaths taken and so on, the parties involved became more confrontational. Ironically it became more difficult for the Magistrate to unravel what really lay behind the given matter which, under the more indirect Chinese practice he was used to, would have emerged. Austin was relieved that in only a few cases that came before him, in the still largely rural New Territories, was there a demand by the parties to resort to English common law.

Although Austin's memoirs are written in an entertaining style, we can sense that despite his making light of it, the job was a demanding one which he took seriously, attempting to defend the traditional way of life in his area of authority. In the end the effort took its toll on his health. On medical advice he was sent away for a month's holiday and on return posted to the Secretariat rather than returning to the New Territories. He was appointed Assistant Colonial Secretary.

While *Myself as Mandarin* maintains a broadly biographical approach, Austin gives fictional form to his Hong Kong life in his novel, *The Road*. At the centre of the ex-patriate web is Sylvia Fairburn, an unlikely character to be found among the dull wives of the colonial civil servants. She is an intelligent, committed writer, if not a conventional one. Her novel, *The Chasm of Love*, while bringing her fame has also caused a scandal as it describes a love affair between a British woman and an Indian attaché in Japan where Sylvia had lived before coming to Hong Kong. Such a theme is grist to the mill of the gossipy ladies like Mrs Webb and Brenda Macpherson, members of the snobbish gang of British expatriates who haunt the cocktail party circuit and are to be found as guests on Government launch picnics. They feign shock that one of their own could write about such a socially disturbing theme, even worse associating with it personally in the way Sylvia has done. Intermingling with the natives was beyond the pale and amounted to a threat to the colonial social order based strict hierarchies, with the British on the top.

Nevertheless, Sylvia's notoriety gives her some status: the Governor himself attends a lecture she gives at the British Council. His arrival, in the sleek, official limousine with pendant flags flying unnerves the British Council official who says that the Governor has never deigned to visit the institution before. Sir Fred is a debonair, relaxed character who enjoys Sylvia's company and senses an underlying tension between her and Richard. On another occasion, they sit on the terrace at Government House conversely amiably while a servant comes with a decanter and glasses before dinner.

Even more dangerous in the eyes of the expatriate ladies is Sylvia's empathy with the Chinese. Before coming to Hong Kong, Sylvia has spent time in China where she has learned Mandarin. Working for the British Army Aid Group in China, she had been in an informal atmosphere in which Europeans and Chinese mingled without any concern. The contrast with the attitudes in Hong Kong could not be more marked. Even though her brown eyes and flowing hair are not thought beautiful by the Chinese, given her ability to speak and even write their language:

*She was one of those special exceptions to the rule about Westerners, the rule being that Westerners were generally disliked. The rule being so, the exceptions were quickly raised to Living Buddha rank, preceded and followed by tales of many marvels.*[viii]

Sylvia is well received by the wealthy Chinese: Frances Lau in one of those circles, embodying Cantonese vitality with Peking breeding. Unconcerned with what the expats think, Frances, who lives in grand style in a mansion on the Peak, greatly admires her Chinese-speaking friend. Frances's character matches that of Trudy in Janice Lee's *The Piano Teacher*; one of the rare breeds of Chinese ladies who are prepared to cross accepted boundaries to have their own way. But Sylvia can also empathise with the simple, country people that live on the island of Lantau where her husband, Richard, is the District Officer. Richard too is not cast in the usual, conventional mould, proclaiming his relief that the law prohibiting Chinese from living on the Peak had been abolished. He sets about, under instructions from the Acting Governor to encourage the villagers to accept that the Governor's pet scheme to build a great road right across the island. The official mantra is once the road is built, prosperity will follow. The villagers will be able to grow vegetables which can be sent to Wireless Bay by road and then to Hong Kong itself in time for the morning market, providing them with a good living. The villagers, whose farms and homes will be destroyed, are not convinced. The idea of new villages being built for them is not something they welcome.

One of the islanders is young Ah Fai, a boy of nineteen whom Richard knows and has already befriended in the past. Ah Fai's main preoccupation is getting to see his heartthrob, Mei Mei, whom he wants to marry instead of the girl, agreed between his family and hers in the age-old practice of arranged marriages. The neighbouring village where Mei Mei lives is most easily reached by boat. Richard obliges by taking him on board the official launch. When Sylvia talks to him as they sail across the azure sea, she learns that the villagers are against the scheme which will end their traditional way of life through fishing, hard though it might seem to an outsider.

However, the momentum for the project grows. When Ah Fai tells the unscrupulous 'Dirty Joke Wong' about it, that fat man with 'fish eyes and a fish mouth'[ix] becomes interested, seeing the possibility of making a killing. He begins to buy up land, banking on its increased value as the scheme goes through. Ah Leung, the chief clerk in Richard's office who echoes the character of Mr Lo, the real-life clerk/interpreter, senses the direction things are going in. He accepts a few bribes to hurry things through; hundred-dollar bills are stacked on his desk in the District Office. Eventually Richard is outflanked and the scheme goes ahead. Rather unfairly, it falls to him to face the villagers when the time comes for their evacuation. The elders meet him, carrying arms and he is backed by the police, also armed. However, with good command of Cantonese, he manages to persuade some of the younger villagers to accompany him to the site of the new houses that have been built for them. There is no further resistance. When the road has been built it is opened with pomp and circumstance by the governor, the displaced villagers lurking in the background.

Austin's novel distils much of what he had learned as magistrate in a rural area of Hong Kong. He shows a great deal of knowledge about how the rural communities work and the mentality of their inhabitants. The neighbouring villages that will be affected by the road scheme are made up of different clans, separated only by some fields and a patch of rough ground. Ah Fai is drawn in very sympathetic colours whilst 'Dirty Joke Wong' represents the unacceptable face of capitalist Hong Kong. Ah Fai is the victim of the traditional, arranged marriage and rebels against it. Details of Chinese etiquette are well drawn: when Ah Fai disagrees with 'Dirty Joke Wong' he begins by reciting the argument he does not believe in. What seems like beating about the bush is a way of saving his opponent's face. What he fails to see is that Ah Leung, the clerk/interpreter in the District Office is in league with 'Dirty Joke Wong' so is unlikely to be sympathetic to Ah Fai's own cause.

On the other side, the colonial elite are mercilessly satirised. One of them, Willie Rogers who has spent much of his career among the Chinese sums up the hopeless gap in understanding their culture:

*To a simple man like myself, and to my men also, anything about the Chinese is so impossibly difficult to explain! For instance, my orderly only this morning was asking me why it's called the Mid-Autumn Festival, when the autumn hasn't even started. And, dammit, I couldn't give him a proper answer. I don't know myself!*[x]

There is tragedy before the dénouement of the story is reached. Ah Fai who has been cast out of his village because of refusing to comply with the elders' plan for the arranged marriage, is given temporary accommodation at the Fairburns' home, in the servants' quarters. However, his behaviour becomes erratic and threatening. When Sylvia calls Interpreter Leung in to try to resolve the difficulty, after some abusive language, Ah Fai suddenly disappears. Ah Fai and Mei Mei enter a suicide pact and their bodies are found near the new reservoir which is part of the development.

Meanwhile, Sylvia and Richard survive an estrangement in their marriage – she goes abroad for a while – but are eventually reconciled. Her flirtation with the Acting Governor amounts to nothing more than that though it has excited much gossip in the expatriate community. But the Fairburns' days in Hong Kong are numbered. Richard is summoned by the Governor and told he is being posted back to the Colonial Office in London, ostensibly to recover after a gruelling time in post on Lantau.

Austin's departure from Hong Kong in 1956 is recorded with a great sense of nostalgia. He his chauffeured to Kai Tak airport after visiting his old office in the Secretariat where everyone is so busy that they have little time to speak to him. He has become a ghost and wonders what he has achieved during his tenure. Soon up in the sky, the airplane flies for a few precious minutes over the area where the Special Magistrate had presided. Peering out of the window, Austin sees a small white spot below which is a bridge enabling village children to cross a river to their school on the other side. Built into the side of the bridge was a large slab of granite, engraved with the names of all those who had subscribed to its construction. The plaque was of a most durable stone and the name at the top of it was Kao Tze, Austin's Chinese name.

Austin's theme about what constitutes 'Chineseness' and the racism inherent in colonial society is taken up in his novel, *City of Broken Promises.* Although the novel is set in Macau in the late eighteenth century, his preoccupations are the same ones – about race and exclusion – as in his writings on Hong Kong. They are part of the same narrative. The story is about the life and loves of Martha Mierop, a Chinese girl abandoned at birth and sold into prostitution who becomes the richest woman merchant on the China coast and a great benefactress. Her lover is an Englishman with a Dutch surname – Thomas van Mierop. He is the son of the founder of Lloyds and related to the philosopher, Jeremy Bentham. Although a successful merchant, he has clear moral scruples and speaks out against the opium trade which was enriching many merchants in Macau.

The story is told against the sometimes-turbulent political background when the Chinese sealed off the border with Macau, threatening it with starvation. At other times restrictions on the movement of all vessels in the Pearl estuary were made. Canton could be suddenly cut off from foreign trade and those residing from overseas ordered to leave. One of the more graphic episodes in the novel is when news comes of the banning of the opium trade which had made various Macau merchants rich. Demand messages from the East India Company (always known as the 'John Company') coinciding with threats from China that anyone found possessing opium would be arrested, sent panic waves through the city. Some merchants buried whatever substance they had in their gardens; others like the leading dealer, Biddles, absconded.

Austin's novel is enhanced by the atmosphere of a decadent Macau which he manages to recreate. Descriptions of the physical surroundings contribute to the sense of decay:

*At the end of the garden, the house looked forlorn and derelict. Some of its plaster had come off in the typhoons of the previous summer. Its black shutters, their paint scarred with the pink they had once been, stood haphazardly, some open, some shut, and one lopsidedly broken at the hinge. A sturdy plant sprouted from the apex of the main gable.[xi]*

But the real interest of the novel is in its vivid portrayal of the complex criss-cross pattern of relationships across the ethnically mixed colony, administered by the Portuguese but watched over by China and, to some extent made prosperous by the enterprise of British merchants. It is the same, mixed background to the society he encounters in Hong Kong. Austin is not sparing of his fellow countrymen as a passage showing how Martha deals with a dishonest member of the British community vividly illustrates:

*Do I have to remind you she went on that you are no longer among the English, where your word is all important and mine means nothing? You have made the mistake the English are always so careful to avoid. You have come down to my level, on which the word of an Englishman means nothing whatever. Do you wish to stay on my level, Mr Cuming, or shall I send you back to your own?[xii]*

The complications of being a half-caste, typical of colonial situations is also explored in the character of Kwan Po, tall for his age with 'soft wavy hair, and grey brown eyes' who when asked his name by Thomas Mierop enquires whether the master wants his Chinese name. Speaking first in Cantonese, he then switches to English 'you may call me Ignatius if you wish.'[xiii] Ignatius is obviously a product of that forbidden breed of Macanese whose father was European and whose mother was Asian. Marriage between the races was strictly forbidden: when an Englishman decided to defy the convention by marrying his local mistress, he was ostracized from society and made to suffer financially, in one case ending up as a street trader. Austin shows that a person of strong personality like Ignatius can overcome the handicap of his mixed background but such individuals are exceptions to the rule. He expresses it powerfully:

*What, for example, would be the future of Pigou's sons, or of any other such child? Neither Portuguese nor Chinese, and certainly not English, born between two worlds, trusted by neither, brought up by illiterate women and thus themselves unlettered, what future could there possibly be for such boys but to become petty criminals of some kind, or one of the elegantly tailored, English-speaking beggars sometimes encountered, hawking their sisters.*[xiv]

The elegance of colonial life is marred by an underlying harshness.

But above all, Austin's exploration of what it is to be Chinese, permeates episodes in Martha's story. At one point led on by the servant Ah Sum, Martha she is forced to don the best *samfoo* of black Shuntak silk, dressing her hair in Chinese style with a pigtail. It was the first time Martha had been dressed in Chinese clothes: only when she looked at herself in the mirror did, she realise that she, who had been brought up to fear the Chinese, was a Chinese girl like any other.

The complicated tapestry of Chinese clan loyalties, arranged marriages and clandestine deals lurks behind Martha's hard journey up the greasy pole, just as it did in the machinations surrounding the building of the road in Lantau in *The Road*. Martha's knowledge of how to deal in the Chinese way, pushing only when it was necessary, ensures her ultimate success.

Austin's sources for *City of Broken Promises* were records which he found extant both in Lisbon and in Macau but also from local, oral traditions which he learned about and which had been handed down from one generation to the next. The stories were gleaned from talking to local Macanese, a technique quite modern at the time. At the same time, he is a master of creating scenes, with an Oriental flavour, such as one of the servants moving about noiselessly in cloth slippers and appearing from the darkness of a porch into the dimly lit house. Other scenes such as those on the streets, reflecting images which George Chinnery has handed down in his sketches, also add to the Chinese atmosphere.

With these fictional portrayals of the Chinese character, we have come full circle on Austin, linking the sharp observations of the Special Magistrate to the flowing prose of the novelist. Unfathomable, opposite, illogical in the eyes of the

Westerner – Chinese cultural attitudes have evolved over millennia conditioning people to behavioural patterns that disguise underlying sentiment and emotion. Austin is not fooled by this cover up; indeed, his keen awareness of it makes him a highly perceptive, as well as entertaining guide, to the Chinese mindset.

# Chapter 2
# A Many-Splendoured Thing: Han Suyin

Although Han Suyin was Eurasian, she identified herself as Chinese despite the fact that, like Timothy Mo, she writes in English. Nevertheless, the dilemma of her mixed background never entirely disappears. As a professional in Hong Kong, she moves in the British colonial circles, accepted because she is a doctor. But it is a provisional acceptance, something tolerated rather than welcomed. Unless they could pass off as Europeans, Eurasians were cast into an in-between category. Like Ignatius in Austin Coates's *City of Broken Promises* or Wallace in Timothy Mo's *Monkey King*, they were outsiders who had somehow to break through the barriers of the society in which they lived. Han Suyin sees being Eurasian as a state of mind forced on a person by the values of colonial society; she does not want to accept that constraint and so chooses to belong to the Chinese side of her heritage.

Han Suyin was born in Xinyang in Henan province of a Chinese father and a Flemish mother. Her first experience of discrimination was at Yenching university. There she discovered that the Chinese rejected Eurasians in the same way as she later found that the British did in Hong Kong. Despite her father's ethnicity, she was not accepted as bona fide Chinese. Her identity crisis had begun. She left to continue her medical studies first in Brussels and later in London. However, after qualifying as a doctor, she returned to China, marrying a Chinese military man (on the Nationalist side) and worked in a mission hospital in Chengdu. That became the setting for her first novel, *Destination Chungking*. During that time, she adopted her daughter, Yungmei.

In 1949 she took up a post in Queen Mary Hospital on Hong Kong Island. In Hong Kong she met and fell in love with Ian Morrison (fictionalised as 'Mark') an Australian reporter with sinophile proclivities who was killed in the Korean War a year later, in 1950. After her Hong Kong period, Han Suyin moved to

Singapore, marrying a British official. It was the time of the Communist insurgency in Malaya so any suspected sympathiser would be watched with suspicion by the authorities. She acted as medical adviser to Nanyang University having turned down an offer to teach literature claiming she wanted to create new writing rather than wallow in the classics. Nanyang University had been established by wealthy Chinese to ensure an education in Mandarin for their children: it was later closed down by Lee Kwan Yew on the suspicion that it was a hotbed of communism. Her experiences in this period are portrayed in the novel, *And the Rain My Drink*. Divorced from her British husband, she married for the third time an Indian colonel and moved to live in Bangladesh, making frequent return visits to Hong Kong.

Han Suyin's time in Hong Kong is immortalised in her novel *A Many-Splendoured Thing* which was also made into a block buster Hollywood movie. The book is a curious blend of autobiography, political commentary and the account of a doomed love affair with 'Mark' the correspondent with whom she had fallen in love. It is set in the same period when, as we have seen, Austin Coates (whom she met) was serving as a magistrate in the New Territories, a time of considerable turmoil, with civil war raging in China and an influx of refugees in Hong Kong which doubled the population of the colony, putting enormous pressure on resources, especially for housing. As a result, people were squashed into tiny cubicles where flimsy partitions divided them from neighbours. While labour was cheap, life was expensive in the booming city.

Han Suyin was not provided with accommodation on her return to Hong Kong to practice medicine so she took up lodgings, with Yungmei, in Church Guest House, run by the missionaries. In her Chengdu days Han Suyin had had contact with missionaries, admiring those who could set aside their *amour-propre* and work hard to help the impoverished masses. Her salary as a doctor was modest; having to support her daughter meant that she had to live frugally. One of her duties as a medical officer involved dispelling a local taboo: she was constantly approached to examine young girls so as to ensure that they were virgins before marriage, something insisted upon by Chinese men.

While the refugees in Hong Kong huddled in their tiny spaces, living on the local gruel, *congee*; entrepreneurs benefitted from the booming business economy, greatly boosted by an influx of Shanghainese businessmen fleeing from the city which had been the cosmopolitan centre of China. These wealthy newcomers established themselves as an elite, frequenting a network of meeting places which included their favourite restaurants and clubs, only rubbing shoulders with the British at official events or in Happy Valley at the races. They regarded themselves as above everyone else including the humdrum British civil servants who purported to run the colony. Their wives enjoyed lapping up all the luxury goods that were flooding into the colony from all over the world.

Among the colonial hierarchy itself were the idle wives of the officials, ladies served by a retinue of servants, with nothing better to do than to gossip about the latest scandal. These pampered creatures were not like Joyce Booth, Martin's mother, with her interest in Chinese culture and in making Chinese friends. Rather they despised the local 'natives' who were prohibited from living on the Peak, their sacrosanct area, where the only Chinese to be seen were their servants. Han Suyin is undoubtedly thinking of them when she says:

*I've never knew such a beautiful place as Hong Kong and I've never known such bloody-minded people.*[xv]

Han Suyin's feeling of alienation as a Eurasian once again comes to the fore. Although she says that Eurasians should feel superior and rejoice in their understanding of two different cultures, her own way out of their dilemma is to deny the European, 'white' side of herself. China unseen, is always felt; it is just beyond the hills of Kowloon even if the majority of the Hong Kong colonial classes behave as if it did not exist. As she puts it:

*I had wanted to be all Chinese, not a counterfeit semi-European, one of those gay, generous people who lived on the brink of the small European circles of Shanghai or Peking, in their curious half-world of concessions and colour bars, a world now dead, like the missions, and the superiority of the whites, and many other things.*[xvi]

This sentiment echoes the experience of Austin Coates's character Kwan Po (whose European name is Ignatius) in *City of Broken Promises* who, despite his defiance in asking whether he should answer in Chinese or English when asked his name by his employer, Thomas Mierop, feels all the insecurity of his ambiguous position in society. Wallace in Mo's *Monkey King,* who at first seems to maintain a slight superiority towards the Chinese because of his drop of European blood soon discovers the same prejudice when he begins his career in the Hong Kong government service. All he can do is to blot out his mixed background in his work environment.

One notion that Han Suyin, like Coates, is also anxious to dismiss is that of the impassive Oriental. She draws on her experience as a doctor to observe:

*The impassive, inscrutable Oriental is another myth. There are no people less reticent, more eager to discuss their physical ailments and their mental interiors than the Chinese. In China one knows everything about everyone else; where, at a certain stage Europeans withhold part of the facts, draw a modest veil over further events, the Chinese carry on, undismayed and unfaltering. There are no unmentionables in China.[xvii]*

Most foreigners do not understand this hidden part of the Chinese character. Sometimes Han Suyin finds that the English are in fact more evasive than the Chinese in expressing any feelings other than ironic, light-hearted expressions of wit. Approaching one English confidante to discuss her affair with Mark, she finds that he only takes a practical view of her situation. There is no empathy with the emotional turmoil that she is experiencing. The clear message is that her affair with a Westerner, though well known to the British community, is best not spoken about.

Han Suyin considers herself to be Chinese patriot. Somewhat disingenuously she claims not to be politically minded but to be motivated solely by her professional calling as a doctor to serve her people. Yet her urge to return to China is not without qualification. She accepts that the Chinese can be every bit as exclusive as the English, exhibiting considerable signs of xenophobia. Nor are hierarchies absent in Chinese society: by long standing tradition the elders in any community control local affairs; in the family their position at the top of the tree is unchallengeable. Moreover, different cultures and languages exist: Han Suyin is told by a voluble Cantonese speaker that, not speaking Cantonese, she does not speak Chinese. She is Shanghainese. When she protests that she is not from Shanghai, the reply comes back pat:

*For us Cantonese, says Mabel, all North is Shanghai. And here Cantonese is Chinese. We don't speak Northern language. So, you don't speak Chinese.[xviii]*

The mix in Hong Kong was particularly complex. In institutions like the hospital where Han Suyin worked, the professors and senior staff were all English while the more junior and students were Chinese. These mainly Cantonese speakers did not wish to rock the boat and annoy their superiors by appearing to sympathise with Communist China. Han Suyin, subscribing to a pro-Communist daily newspaper, was a suspicious character and ostracised by them.

Moreover, the Hong-Kong born resented the influx of the energetic and well-qualified Shanghainese who threatened their own position in the colonial hierarchy. These locals, caught between different worlds, had a different attitude to British rule than the mainlanders coming into the colony. They supported the status quo which offered them some protection and security. In her enthusiasm for the mother country, Han Suyin failed to understand that the well-established Hong Kong classes would not, in fact, welcome a return to China. Whatever social limitations existed in the colony, they could be submerged in the mix and left to get on with making money, a major preoccupation in Hong Kong. A Chinese take over in which they could be targeted as 'running dogs', filled them with dread.

Han Suyin was much influenced by her cousin Sen who persuades her that the Communist Revolution is an opportunity to lift the masses, with millions on the edge of starvation, out of their dire poverty. The Revolution is a spiritual struggle as well as a material one, led by idealists:

*To the communist, each individual was a fortress to be taken by spiritual struggle alone. That the struggle involved sleepless nights and physical strain was added proof of spiritual superiority. They were out to conquer souls, and bodies would follow.*[xix]

And in their relentless efforts the young idealist did not appear to need food or sleep; they were willing to give up their lives for the cause. Their efforts represent the chance to build a new China where the best traditions of Confucianism would continue, where poets would still wax lyrical about the moon but in which there would be far greater equality among its subjects. That objective could only be achieved with the removal of the Kuomintang and its corrupt links to Western interests. Later Han Suyin accepts that these ideals were shattered by the Cultural Revolution; scientists and intellectuals were protected only while Chou En Lai was still in power. Friends of hers suffered persecution and early death during that turbulent period. She estimates that probably a million people were either executed or locked up for long periods of imprisonment.

In Hong Kong Han Suyin is also struck by the huge inequalities that exist: it is impossible for her to ignore the contrast of extreme affluence and dire poverty, cheek by jowl, in the crammed territory as more and more refugees flood in. Most of these arrive penniless and get into the hands of gangs of racketeers. Everything is up for sale: women, gold, medicines, passports and visas. The illegal operations are oiled along by corruption among officials. It is not an edifying sight as we shall see Lin Tai Yi describing in *Kampoon Street.*

Han Suyin does not disguise her desire to return to China, according to her, not because of being a Communist but because she is Chinese and because the Revolution promises to improve the dire lot of the majority of the population. Her situation in Hong Kong, with all its advantages, still leaves her feeling alienated. She is not a full member of either the British or the Chinese community. Her sympathy with the revolution in China and her subscription to a pro-Communist newspaper, earns her the title of 'The Red Doctor'. It is an anomalous position for someone of her status to be in.

Nevertheless, she continues to move in exclusive circles. In her more directly biographical account, *My House has Two Doors* (1982) she recalls her friendship with the Governor, Sir Alexander Grantham, whose good humour is also mentioned by Martin Booth in *Gweilo.* She clearly admires Grantham to whom she ascribes a sense of history and an idea of the impermanence of the very colony over which he presides. The Governor seems to be drawn to her because he senses that, unlike many of the people he comes in contact with, she shares his foreboding about the future in which the colonial structure will be swept away. That feeling of the intransigence seems to bind them together; there is a hint too that she finds the tall, debonair Englishman attractive as no doubt he does the glamorous Eurasian doctor.

The 'Red Doctor' is invited to Government House on a regular basis and even shares the Governor's box at the races in Happy Valley. When there is a delay and even a suggestion that her request to obtain a British passport might be refused, Grantham steps in and sends a written instruction to his subordinates to get on with her application, no doubt written in the red ink that only he was allowed to use. The background to the passport application is amusingly related to her by Austin Coates, who has become a friend, over tea no doubt in a venue like the lounge of the Gloucester Hotel:

*My dear, you should have seen the files on you! His hands curved up and down in a pyramid of files. A Red, a pro-communist, a fellow traveller! The Special Branch was just going to turn you down when they got a little note, a little note, my dear, from HE himself! About you. What is happening about Dr Han's naturalisation? I would like to see it dealt with quickly... My dear, Special Branch almost collapsed.*[xx]

And then Austin Coates, whom she describes as 'an art connoisseur, a collector of antiques',[xxi] as well as a mere government servant, broke into giggles.

Later when she is about to marry Leonard, she chooses a remote chapel in Pokfulam for the ceremony. The Granthams are invited but so that the Governor's car can be driven right up to the door of the chapel, a proper road has to be laid weeks in advance. After the ceremony over a hundred guests are invited to a reception at the Hong Kong Hotel. Having had to save up for the expense of such a lavish gathering, Han Suyin is nevertheless pleased that anyone who was anyone, including the Governor and his wife, turned up. After all she had been affected by the need for status in Hong Kong society.

The charmed colonial circles in which Han Suyin moved involved cocktails and dinner parties on the Peak attended by the same gossiping ladies who were determined to do her down. Their hostility towards her is palpable: how could this Chinese woman, with clear Communist sympathies, have infiltrated the highest levels of their society? How did she ensnare the charming young journalist? One or two of these ladies loom larger than life in the narrative; some are less stuck up than others.

She is at first put off by a certain Adeline Palmer-Jones, married to an influential business tycoon. Mrs Palmer-Jones is on every board and committee making decisions about social services; nothing is done without her agreement. Snidely remarking that Mrs Palmer-Jones cannot forget that she was a mere missionary in an earlier life, Han Suyin nevertheless accepts an invitation to dinner for a favoured few after the Palmer-Jones's annual cocktail party, an event of considerable social importance in the colony. A fellow guest remarks that in Hong Kong one tended to stick to one's known circle of friends while Adeline

Palmer-Jones is brave enough to mix people from all groups together. Han Suyin accepts that this is the case although she is still critical of the majority of the upper echelons of Hong society, including Old China hands who do not deign to learn anything from the locals. She says in a bitter tone:

*All the ingredients were there, ready for the mixing. The melting-pot of the Orient, they called Hong Kong. Indeed no. The place where everyone met and many stayed apart, divided by hedges of prejudice and hearsay. However much one shook the mixture, it stratified in to immiscible layers again.[xxii]*

Whatever Han Suyin thought of Hong Kong society, her delight in the physical beauty of the environment is palpable in all her descriptions.

*Hong Kong was a delight; the piercing blue sky; the reflecting, crystal merry sea we crossed and re-crossed by ferry to Kowloon to hear the gurgle and suck of water under the boat and feel the mild, cool wind upon our faces.[xxiii]*

It is the island itself that particularly charmed her:

*I walked up the slopes of Victoria Island, up Conduit Road. Poinsettias in pots spread their carmine explosions atop the stone walls which banked old and graceful villas. The ladder street escalating slopes, innumerable tiny shops open day and night...[xxiv]*

When she pays a visit to the Botanical Gardens, she paints a calm picture of the university spreading out on the hillside below with a clear view of the harbour, busy with ships and local craft. In the distance the bare hills of Kowloon are visible and beyond them, the great mystery that is China. Like Martin Booth her reaction to the Peak itself was mixed. Like him while admiring the panoramic views of the harbour from its steep eminence, she cannot escape the feeling that this is a place reserved for the few, the entrenched hierarchy of the Colony's society. Its lofty summits are the bastions of retreat for the great merchant princes (*taipans*) who lived there in grand style. Prominent among them were the heads of the firm of Jardine Matheson: an invitation to their homes was more sought after than one to Government House.

She was more at ease on the beaches, both at Deep Water Bay and Repulse Bay where young Yungmei, increasingly Westernised, delighted in swimming, chewing her bubble gum and drinking her Watsons orangeade after her dip in the warm sea. At Deep Water Bay they enjoyed the hospitality of a wealthy Australian friend whose sumptuous house was on the water's edge. Inside the house was a collection of rare antiques and works of art including the disturbing painting of a Chinese coolie, portrayed in his rags, insolently extending his twisted hand, in a begging motion. It was an immediate reminder of the poverty and destitution in the city beyond.

A vivid account is given of a visit, with a group of friends to Aberdeen and its floating restaurants. The visitors are mobbed by a surging crowd of boat women, dressed in traditional black trousers with aprons over them and round straw hats on their heads. They vie with one another to get the group to step into their own sampan which will ferry them across to the floating restaurant. One boat woman, more abrasive than the others, manages to push her way forward and soon Han Suyin and her friends are seated on the rattan chairs on her sampan. Coloured paper lanterns, marking the Moon Festival, adorn the boat while the floating restaurant is lit up with gaudy neon signs.

The crashing of mahjong cubes, always played during festivals, assails their ears as they reach the side of the restaurant barge. Greeted by a sleek, young manager they seek a table which will give them a view of the moon. Large wooden pens are fixed to the side of the ship in which swim the fish that the customers will choose. Round baskets are stuffed with lobsters, crabs and squid. A team of expert cooks stand ready on a floating platform. A young boy deftly scoops out the fish they want; the first cook stuns it and passes it to the second who, with a single swipe, slices it in half. He passed it on to the next and eventually at the end of the line the finely decorated fish emerges on a porcelain platter.

Another enjoyable occasion is the celebrations that herald in Chinese New Year. Weeks beforehand, shops laden with food and luxury goods from all over the world, are raided by families intent on seeing in the new year in style. Amid the imported chocolate boxes and bottles of brandy, are Chinese dehydrated and flattened ducks, entire suckling pigs and rows of red and white sausages hanging from the shop ceilings. On the day itself the noise of firecrackers, some hung in long strings on the side of buildings, is deafening. The streets turn into rivers of red paper and cinders; everything smells of roast pork and gunpowder.

Han Suyin's romance with Mark in *A Many-Splendoured Thing* is told very much in a physical setting, if an unusual one. Below Queen Mary Hospital where she was working, there was a mortuary, a small concrete structure shaded by bamboo and sheltered from the road below by a hibiscus hedge. A paved path led along the hillside for several miles to some water reservoirs, situated just above the university slopes. In the lane (known as 'Lovers Lane') there was a large, flat stone ledge. This was taken over by the couple. While Han Suyin rushed down from the hospital, Mark came up the steep rise from Pokfulam Road. Seated on their stone, at times in the early hours of the morning, they had panoramic views:

*We could talk, hold hands, look at the galaxies of the fishing fleets toiling the sea, the River of Heaven rolling its innumerable splendid sails above our heads. The moon was often with us, an affable companion, casting her pale blue glow on our faces and on the stones of the Chinese cemetery opposite the Hospital. At least for a few minutes, nearly every night, we could see each other, assuaging our avidity in passionate restraint, talking in low voices, more often silent, Mark holding the little finger of my right hand; teaching each other all the time. The mortuary was a good place to meet.* [xxv]

One of the escapes that the couple make is to Macau where they enjoy some light-hearted moments as Bunt and Mei-ping are to do in Theroux's *Kowloon Tong*. The gambling houses provide the spectacle of every type of person; the grotto of Camões and the promenade along the Praia Grande on the sea shore are suitably romantic in the evening light. As they see Macau slipping away from the deck of the departing ferry; Han Suyin falls into a slumber, watched over by an adoring Mark. As she allows herself to be swept away by their mutual adoration, doubts remain. Not only is Mark married but how are they ever going to be accepted in a society which frowns on mixed marriages?

A constant theme in the narrative is the enchantment with the moon, something to be found throughout Chinese literature. She and Mark are fixated by the moon as she tells us in lyrical prose:

*We called ourselves amiable lunatics, pervaded by moonbeam madness, fervent disciples, docile unfettered captives no longer disputing our surrender to her enchantment. In Europe saints have called themselves the fools of God, and worn the livery of triumphant ecstasy; in China poets have become the lovers of the moon, and one of them lost his earthbound life attempting to embrace her in a lake.*[xxvi]

Mark himself recalls travelling through Sumatra by night with guides and elephants bathed in moonlight as they waded through the tall grass. He favours the Spring moon, quoting the Chinese poet who described the hill tops lit up as if they were white jade while Han Suyin prefers the Autumn Moon. In the evenings from their stone near the mortuary, the couple watch the moon, orange and opaque, shining onto the foliage of the slopes around. With a view of the sea in the distance, the effect transfixes them.

Recording a moon anthology of their own, Han Suyin discussed the poetry of the Tang poet Li Po with her circle of intellectual friends that included John Tam, Dr Goh, François Perrin (a young Frenchman) and the Jesuit priest, Father Low who was well versed in Chinese literature. She liked the legend that Li Po had drowned while trying to clutch the moon on a boat. Whether it actually happened or not was always a subject of dispute among scholars but it has had no effect on the popularity of the legend. While Father Low wished that Li Po's life might have been given for a better cause, François Perrin regarded his death, clutching his beloved moon in his arms, to be the very best way to leave the earth.

On the trip that she made with her friends to the floating restaurant in Aberdeen, a dramatic moment occurs involving the moon. The clouds had been hanging over the sky blocking out the moon. The fisher people around started to beat gongs loudly and set off firecrackers. Suddenly the clouds shifted and the moon broke through:

*Solitary she stood, feline and glaring, the liquid light pouring from her, so beautiful, the autumn moon, and we forever caught by her beauty. The fishermen cheered; the children clapped their hands while the baffled cloud tore its last shreds away pursued by a final jeering crepitation of crackers. We now called for another cattie of hot yellow wine to toast the moon.*[xxvii]

A more complex aspect of Chinese cultural influence on Han Suyin is the interweaving of Confucian and Taoist principles. Confucianism (which she says is so respected by the English) teaches the moral virtues, particularly of tolerance and respect although Han Suyin claims that it never quelled the exuberant and

42

vital spirit in the Chinese character. It sees man as a social being whose ideal is that he should lead the good life, cultivated under the direction of virtuous government. Taoism, on the other hand, opposes nature to man, glorifying Tao (or the way) as a journey in which emptiness and tranquillity will play an important part of man's enlightenment. Both are significant strands in Chinese thought. In Han Suyin, Confucianism is linked to the notion of greater fairness in society, of replacing a corrupt regime in China with one that respects individuals and their happiness. That is the way she looks upon the Communist Revolution and why she claims not to be political. Her Taoism consists in her love of nature; her pursuit of silence and open spaces that forms a background to the way she sees her romance with Mark.

Intertwined with that tendency is her aestheticism: she searches for and finds beauty in the mundane; immortality is best put on hold because beauty is so mortal, so tangible. Daily scenes remind her of spiritual beauty: the song and sight of wagtail and laughing thrush, the chorus of golden oriole at dawn. Moments of rapture transport her into the world of the artist; the underlying theme of love, a many-splendoured thing, sharpens her sensibility.

This mixture of thinking brings us back to the essential dilemma facing Han Suyin. Her Eurasian ethnicity and European education (leading to her writing, as she does, in English) contrast with her desire to be a Chinese patriot with a profound commitment to Chinese cultural values. She talks of moving at different times, in different worlds. Seeing her off at Kai Tak airport on her return visit to Chunking, Mark has a sense of foreboding about what might happen when she is back in China, seeing things with Chinese eyes. Would she re-assess their relationship and decide to give it up?

When Han Suyin first arrives in Chungking, she cannot banish thoughts of Hong Kong. Getting into the city from the airport is a laborious business involving hours of travelling along broken roads. The officials at the customs barrier are sullen and unfriendly, a far cry from the happy and well-fed mood of their counterparts in Hong Kong. It is an inauspicious start in the place that she once regarded as home. But soon she says:

*And then the transformation occurred, and the Hong Kong me was gone, it had vanished, dissolved like a cloud in one's hand, and I had never left this place.*
*xxviii*

43

Nevertheless, although she feels once again part of her extended family in China, she does not re-settle and an ambiguous air hangs over her comments on the changes, some better and some worse, that have come upon the city in her long absence. Relations with 'Fifth Brother' are warm while her sister's behaviour, refusing to be part of the inner family circle, makes her share in the family's collective shame. In the end she must break convention herself and tackle her sister headlong about her rupture with the family and her reasons for leaving home to live on her own.

She sees all around her changes that have come about since her own time as a resident; there is a sense of foreboding about the future. It is as if the city has already given up to surrender although some last vestiges of the old, despotic regime continue. There is a daily round up of those suspected of being Communist infiltrators with grisly, public executions. Among the victims were even children who were branded as collaborators. The atmosphere is tense and threatening. Even so the Chinese reaction to disaster, to laugh, is ever present: Fifth Brother makes light of all that has happened, dwelling on the fact that they themselves, he and Han Suyin, have not changed after all the years of separation. And when the Communists do finally take over, there will be great improvements. The river would be dredged, the fields would be drained, trees would be planted on the bare slopes. Much of this work would be carried out by the energetic Youth cadres. By contrast Hong Kong would seem dull and suburban.

When she did return there, moving in colonial circles, the dilemma is sharpened for the 'Chinese lady' who enjoys the benefits of a foreign and alien-dominated society, based on cheap, Chinese labour. Despite her anxiety about the poverty around her, she nevertheless frequents the best places – the luxurious hotels, the air-conditioned cinemas, the beaches which foreigners frequent. To complicate matters further she falls in love with a Westerner (a *gweilo*), freely and frequently admitting that she adores his deep, blue eyes. But her relationship with him is secretly despised by the very society in which she is mixing:

*But at the moment we were vulnerable, we could be hurt. My many-splendoured thing would be smeared across the lips of the complacent and the righteous, thrust at with daggered hints in meanings where hearsay blossomed; fouled with innuendoes and muddied with moralities.*[xxix]

The story ends with a poignant series of letters that Mark pens to Han Suyin from Korea where he has been sent to report on the war. It is an unpleasant assignment where the Americans fight a rear-guard action as they are beaten back southwards. Civilians who get in the way of the crossfire are slaughtered mercilessly by both sides. Mark tries to maintain a detachment but he cannot in the face of the brutality that can include killing entirely defenceless people, the old people and very young who have not fled their villages. Now and again, he succeeds in getting the soldiers to hold their fire but those are isolated victories in a generally bloody campaign. Conditions are dire for the reporters: they usually sleep on the floor of any building still left standing, hygiene is poor, diarrhoea becomes common among them. And the letters constantly return to the theme of whether he and Han Suyin will ever meet again. Holding onto to hope against hope, in his heart Mark doubts that they will. The letters, eighteen in all are delivered day by day until eventually there is a silence.

Han Suyin looks back to the happy time when the two lovers were in Macau, unusually relaxed and free from the constraints that hang over them in Hong Kong. Mark, seeing some acquaintances at a nearby restaurant table, says that he wants everyone to ask who the beautiful Chinese girl is that he is taking out. She corrects him saying she is Eurasian but he tells her that she looks entirely Chinese to him. That is prejudice she retorts but he chides her for not being proud of her dual mind, her great advantage of moving between different cultures. Mark is genuine in saying this but he is in a minority among the colonial elite who tolerate rather than embrace her as one of their own.

If Austin Coates carries something Chinese within himself, Han Suyin carries something Western and inescapable in herself.

# Chapter 3
# Gweilo: Martin Booth

The bustling, post-war period of Hong Kong is vividly captured by Martin Booth in *Gweilo* (foreign devil), his autobiographical account of schoolboy days at the end of the 1940s and the beginning of the 1950s. Although all the colonial trappings are there – tea at the Peninsula, parties in the officers' mess (his father was a middle ranking official in the Naval Service) and even an interview with the Governor, His Excellency, Sir Alexander Grantham, at Government House – it is an unusual story because of young Martin's engagement in Chinese culture, encouraged by his Sinophile mother, Joyce.

In a note prefacing the book, Martin tells the reader that he never intended to write an autobiography since he was not a rock star, explorer, footballer or member of a miscreant aristocracy. He had never kept a diary. The motivation for writing his memoir was to leave a record of his early childhood for his own children as he had been diagnosed with a fatal form of brain cancer so was not left with many years to live. That authorial statement must warn the reader that the past will, to some extent, be seen through rose-tinted spectacles. Some of the detailed observations are unlikely to have been recorded by a boy of eight; the writing style, moreover, is that of a mature, skilled master of the craft. But what he does add, poignantly, is that he feels he never really left Hong Kong: it was his home during his formative years and it is where his roots are.

The narrative begins as the P &O liner, the Corfu, sails out of Southampton and England becomes 'a small but thin line on the darkening horizon.'[xxx] Martin's parents, destined for the comfortable life of ex-patriate colonial servants, are an incompatible pair. Ken, his father, is a truculent and unadventurous time-server; Joyce is a lively, sociable lady full of interest and curiosity about the exotic world which they are entering. On board the ship life follows a comfortable routine: deck quoits in the morning, afternoon on deckchairs reading or sleeping and evenings in the cocktail lounge before dinner. Children were expected to attend school classes in the nursery, decorated with Disney and fairy-tale characters. In the 'imperial' ports along the way, Joyce is excited to see everything in a bright light which contrasts with the gloom of post-war England. In Algiers, against her husband's wishes, she leads an expedition to the *suq*, stopping to sample fresh dates amid the stalls crammed with ceramics, metal ware and spices piled high, with the smoke from hookahs filling the air. In Egypt the target is the Simon Artz Department store, selling alabaster Nefertiti heads. In Colombo they are at Mount Lavinia; in Singapore they speed through the checkpoints set up in the Emergency. Joyce's only reservation seems to be over Bombay which she finds oppressive because of the street beggars whom she pities.

Their arrival in Hong Kong, sailing past some surprisingly green shoreline, is auspiciously greeted by the noon-day gun fired from Jardine Lookout. The Booths' stop – and indeed it became something of a home – was the Four Seasons Hotel in Waterloo Road, Kowloon. The *Sei Hoi Jaudim*, to give it its Chinese name, housed a curious mixture of residents that included colonial servants, like the Booths, waiting for housing, passing American salesmen and, on the top floor, a gaggle of prostitutes waiting for customers. It was situated near enough to the bustling areas of Mong Kok and Yau Ma Tei for young Martin to begin his wanderings around the backstreets of the city. He soon discovered that having fair hair was an immediate passport to acceptance as the locals believed that by stroking his golden locks, they would bring themselves good luck. Usually he was accompanied by Ching, one of the hotel staff whose family, like so many others of the period, had fled to Hong Kong on the defeat of Chiang Kai Shek and the victory of the Communist forces. Ching, like Ah Lan with Malcolm, made sure that Martin was protected from too much stroking of his head as they wandered through the backstreets but he could not protect the youngster from hearing the racy Cantonese idiom which was part of the daily life of the coolies, van drivers and tradesfolk of those streets. Back at the hotel, his *amah* Ah Choy had become a great favourite; he permitted her to undress and wash him. She and other *amahs* had remained loyal to their employers, at some danger to themselves, during the Japanese occupation. Ah Choy looked after Martin as if he were her own child.

One of Martin' favourite haunts were the *dai pai dongs* or canteen restaurants running a 'vibrant trade, steam or charcoal smoke redolent with odours of frying rising from them to the glimmer in neon above'.[xxxi] He and Joyce soon take to Cantonese cuisine whereas his father, Ken, prefers to stick with the ex-patriate nosh served up in such venues as the China Fleet Club, established by British NCOs and ratings. Nevertheless, they avoided some local dishes, such as black dog. The streets around the hotel are highly colourful – unlicensed street hawkers sell sweetmeats, sugar cane, melon seeds and *wah mui*, (sour plums) which had been soaked in sea water and dried. Other vendors carry braziers on poles, selling roasted peanuts, chestnuts, and slices of hot roast pork with crackled skin still on the meat. The last era of the rickshaw on the streets of Kowloon was drawing to an end in the 1950s. Pulled along by coolies wearing conical hats, it was easy for the passenger to slide off as the rickshaw jolted forward and then to be thrown backwards as the coolie picked up the shafts and set off.

In the cool of the evening's night entertainers joined the throng of people milling around in the streets of Kowloon. Brightly-lit pawn brokers shops, placed between restaurants and other stands, threw open their doors. The pavements were lined with stalls selling every conceivable kind of food, as well as clothing and household goods. Entertainers joined the throngs of people wandering in the streets, some in pyjamas, unable to sleep in their stuffy tenement rooms. It was as if the whole city had woken up from its afternoon slumber. Joyce was particularly fond of a shop run by Mr Chan.

*The interior of the shop was like a treasure cave. Heavy Chinese furniture stood piled piece upon piece to the ceilings, layers of cardboard protecting them from marking each other. Glass cabinets contained cloisonné trinkets, ebony carvings, ivory figures and beads, trays of gold rings set with multi-coloured stones, displays of unmounted gems, gold chains, pendants and brooches. One display case was filled with netsuke, another with jade miniatures and Chinese snuff bottles, Siamese silver and enamel fingernail covers and models of junks.* [xxxii]

In the middle of this jumble of things, Mr Chan served tea or cold drinks on a small table. He became Joyce's favourite jeweller.

Just off Nathan Road Martin finds the temple of Tin Hau, the goddess who protects seafarers. He learns that in the ancient legend, she rescued her father and brothers from being shipwrecked in a typhoon, in that way earning her status as a deity. Her image, with Ming headdress and flowing pearls is at the centre of the altar, with the image of lesser beings, one of whom was a wily, old general who could forecast the weather at sea. Offerings are placed in front of the altar; the scent of lighted joss sticks filled the air. Outside fortune tellers and necromancers and phrenologists wait for potential customers who have come to worship the goddess.

Another spectacle to be seen on the streets was elaborate funeral processions. A truck adorned with paper flowers and bunting carried the coffin. The name of the deceased was written in huge characters at the front. Behind it were delivery tricycles similarly adorned. Young men, carrying tall poles topped by Chinese fringe umbrellas, walked in between the vehicles, decorated with large paper figures. The mourners, led by the young son of the deceased, were dressed in white. However young, the son would now have to be head of the family in the absence of his father. Behind the leading truck a band of musicians followed, plying classical music of a dirge like, Chinese type. Another band followed playing Western music jarringly.

These scenes lead Martin to observe that although Hong Kong was beginning to expand – as Austin Coates had seen – into a world financial centre 'it was still essentially a Chinese city with bicycle and a non-interventionist British administration'.[xxxiii] While the Central district saw the rise of some of the tallest buildings in the world (in particular the Bank of China), the shoe shine boys, no doubt followers of Timothy Mo's Ricky, squatted on the pavements with their box in front of them waiting for businessmen or officials passing by.

*If a customer halted, tins of polish, brushes and cloths would appear from within the box. Deft fingers rolled up trouser legs and, within minutes, the shoes would appear pristine, scuff marks and dust removed.*[xxxiv]

By contrast, the streets of Mong Kok and Yau Ma Tei still thronged with coolies carrying heavy loads on bamboo poles and Hakka women wearing hats with black cloth fringes that hung down from the rim. It was a scene that would not greatly differ from one that might have been seen in any mainland city.

One of the most colourful characters eking out a living in a tenement block was 'the Queen of Kowloon'. She was a white Russian refugee, one of the diasporas that had fled her native land at the time of the Bolshevik Revolution. The outbreak of civil war in China forced the emigrants to make for Hong Kong, with its relative security, in the 1930s. At first the 'Queen of Kowloon' made a living from giving piano lessons but in due course, succumbing to alcohol and eventually to opium, she began her descent into destitution. She would appear in the pawn shops of Kowloon selling off family heirlooms – mostly pieces of jewellery or gold coins from the Tsarist period. These transactions roused the interest of criminals; the tenement she lived in was raided a number of times but nothing was ever found there even though the burglars even smashed down internal walls. Clearly the 'Queen' had hidden her valuables elsewhere; living on the edge for years had sharpened her survival instinct. There were various rumours about what had happened to her during the Japanese occupation of Hong Kong. One theory was that she had fled to Macau, spared invasion because of the neutrality of Portugal in the war.

In later years, riddled with opium, her mental condition deteriorated. She claimed to be Princess Anastasia, the only member of the Russian royal family to escape execution by the Bolsheviks. Martin recounts a frightening encounter with her:

*I was trapped by her in a dead-end alley. She advanced on me slowly, her every step measured as if she were tiptoeing from stone to stone across a river. All the while, she was muttering incomprehensibly. Finally, not two yards away, and certainly close enough for me to be swathed in her odour in the windless alley, she stopped and studied me closely.*

*"Why do you run, Alexei?" she asked in English.*
*"My name is not Alexei," I replied.*
*She smiled at me. Her teeth were grey. For a moment a shard of beauty she must once have been shone through her decrepitude.*
*"One day, you will be Tsar," she prophesied.* [xxxv]

Dodging her bad breath and rank smell, he managed to escape but not before she patted him on the head, something that totally unnerved him and turned him violently against her.

Sometime later he saw her for the last time in no less pitiable a condition. By then his dislike of her had subsided and he felt nothing but pity for her. She was being been chased along the road by a store owner with a stiff broom who accused her of stealing. When Martin offered to help her by paying for the stolen fruit, she rushed away from him screaming that he was a devil. Finding his way to her tenement to see if he could help her, all trace of her had gone. A Chinese family was installed in the space she used to occupy.

Another dodgy character in the narrative is Jim, a debauched Englishman eking out his days in the Four Seasons Hotel, seldom emerging from his room. On the occasion when he did, it was to try to lure Martin into sex by showing him a revolver which he had stowed away since his time in the war. Martin decided not to tell his mother about the incident but confided in Ah Ching who, with a posse of other hotel servants, gave Jim a beating as punishment for his behaviour.

Two forbidden areas of Kowloon that Martin frequented were the shanty town at Ho Man Tin and the Walled City. The shanty town was a squatters' area not far from Waterloo Road situated on a hill. Most of the constructions there were made of wood with improvised roofs, patched together with any material at hand but making the makeshift homes highly susceptible to fire. Every kind of activity could be found in the alleyways – some food vendors were steaming off the flesh of fish to make fish balls; others roasting a whole pig on charcoal stoves. The far-haired *gweilo* was received in a friendly fashion by the amused old ladies who handed him boiled sweets.

One day, returning from school, Martin became aware of smoke billowing from the squatters' hill nearby. Throwing down his school bag in the hotel, he rushes up to investigate. The scene that confronts him is one of utter destruction: the make shift huts are blazing in an uncontrollable inferno. Without a thought of the risk to himself, Martin rushes forward to help a family who are trying to salvage their possessions. It is a young family with a child. He wraps up some of their possessions and stumbles down the hill with them. The grateful father follows Martin to the police line where Joyce has been summoned to tell her what a brave boy her son is.

His exploration of the Walled City was even more unusual. This was an enclave left out of the territory handed over to the British. It was virtually an independent little state run by a local mafia. Although occasionally raided by the Hong Kong police, it was not directly administered by the colonial authority allowing it to flourish as a hideout and a haven for criminal activity. Entering with some trepidation but also excitement, Martin faces a threatening tattooed figure who nevertheless listens to his Cantonese greeting and agrees to take him on a 'look-see' or tour. In its maze of alleyways and old temples, reminiscent of China of the Ching dynasty, opium dens and stores crammed with stolen goods were hidden. All the interiors Martin entered were blanketed in a gloom – in the temple a thick fog arose from burning incense; in another room he could just discern a lying figure with the long opium pipe next to him on the divan. There was little contact with anyone and no casual conversations as he was used to on the streets of Kowloon. Martin's guide swears him to secrecy about the visit which he never reports to his parents.

Less exotic was a trip made to the New Territories in his father's gleaming new car about which Ken was obsessive. The family drove out to Sha Tin, then a fishing village on the shores of an inlet with distant views of "Amah's Rock" a formation that in silhouette looked like a woman carrying a baby on her back. They stopped for coffee at the Sha Tin Dairy Farm restaurant, an American-style diner with a pretentious menu although, in the local way, everything including salad, was served with rice. The circular route they followed took them out to Fan Ling (famous for its golf course) close to the border with China. This is Austin Coates's territory – the rural hinterland where peasants in conical hats using buffaloes worked in the fields, once again evoking images of Ching dynasty China. On another occasion in the same area, this time arriving by train with Joyce to attend Ch'ing Ming celebrations with Chinese friends Martin observes:

*The train trundled through Kowloon and entered a tunnel in the hills. When it emerged in the Sha Tin valley, it was as if I was riding a time machine. At one end of the tunnel was a mid-twentieth century city, on the other a timeless landscape of tiny villages, paddy fields, salt pans and fishing junks. If a British man-o'-war had sailed into the cove, cannons blazing, it could still have been the Opium War.[xxxvi]*

Nearby was a traditional cemetery – a narrow ledge cut into the hillside with rows of urns and large, inverted dishes for offerings to the spirits of ancestors. Joss sticks were lit; Joyce and Martin joined in the kow-towing to ancestors. After that a feast of whole suckling pig, warm rice from a thermos and rice wine were served.

On another escape from the city, the family visited Lantau where Martin is fascinated by the old villages, some of which date back a century or more. At Tung Chung the low buildings look across a valley of paddy fields, the edges shaded by banyan, paper bark and lychee trees. Huge yellow bamboo formed the backdrop to the houses, planted by the villagers to attract snakes and rats that would do a good job exterminating each other. Elsewhere the houses had black-tiled roofs; a large suckling pig might be found strewn across the main street.

A more unusual Sunday afternoon was spent visiting the leper colony on the island of Hei Ling Chou. Joyce had read that visitor would be taken there as part of a naval exercise to help the diseased people and that there was no danger of contagion from 'dry' lepers. Martin's father raised serious objections but Joyce was determined and would not be put off. On arrival at the island the family found British personnel running a fun fair to entertain and support the locals. The sight of the lepers with injuries on their hands and faces and, in some cases, with missing limbs moved the young Martin. He allowed one leper to stroke his hair for good luck which earned him a beating from his sadistic father when they returned home.

Martin's life as a backstreet boy in Kowloon came to a sudden end when the Booths were allocated an apartment in Mount Austin, on the Peak. The Peak, a dominating backcloth with the city sprawled out below it on Hong Kong Island, was still a preserve of the British, colonial elite. By regulation Chinese, unless in the employ of Europeans were not permitted to rent property or to live on its misty edges. Mount Austin rose steeply from top Peak Tram terminal so that spectacular views of the harbour could be seen from the apartments. Martin describes the panorama to be seen from the balcony of their new home:

*First the western harbour approaches with merchant vessels awaiting a docking birth or discharging cargo into junks and flat barges called lighters. In the distance was Stonecutters' Island, a military signals base. Further on Kowloon came into sight, the peninsula crammed with buildings, ships lying along the jetties, ferries ploughing across to the island, walla-walla boats little more than aquatic insects. In another hundred yards the central business district and the eastern suburbs came into view, the lower slopes of the hills dotted with houses and the red-brick block of the Bowen Road military hospital. Beyond Kowloon were the nine dragon hills.*[xxxvii]

Much though these sights enthralled Martin, in his high-up perch he felt isolated. It was a far cry from the crowded backstreets of Kowloon which he had become accustomed to roaming around.

He was enlisted in the Peak School, a predominantly British primary school located not far from the Booths' new home. Martin did not feel comfortable there – only a few Chinese from wealthy families and some American and European expatriate children offered any diversity. Discipline was strict and participation in team sports expected of the pupils neither of which appealed to the wandering minstrel that Martin had become. When it was noticed that Martin did not join in games, Joyce was summoned by the Headmistress to discuss the matter. Shirking sports was not regarded as a good omen for character building.

What the Peak did offer him was a closer exploration of nature. Still sparsely populated, the banks and ridges of the mountain were dense with trees and shrubbery. There were steep paths that led down the sides to Pokfulam and the south side of the island, full of bird and animal life. Finding some of the slopes too steep to clamber up, Martin still managed to walk right around the Peak by taking the so-called 'Governor's Walk'.

In the other direction he came upon the Pinewood Battery, a gun platform destroyed during the Japanese invasion of 1941 but with its old structure of command post, ammunition building and sleeping quarters with metal bunks, still intact. This was a purpose-built adventure playground. In the slopes below, exotic animals like the muntjac and the ferret badgers could be found while on the shores of the bay below were turtles. However, walking down the hillside to favourite beaches could be dangerous: snakes could be lurking in the wide *nullahs* or drains that siphoned off water from torrential downpours of rain. The Peak of that time was still a semi-tropical jungle. Martin found it particularly enchanting when the mist swirled in, covering everything in a damp layer. Walking down Mount Austin, he would pass a deserted tram terminal, usually thronging with tourists. Along the path on the way to school, he hardly encountered a single person.

At other times, when the skies were clear, the modest Peak Café, the only establishment offering refreshment was invaded by tourists including American sailors who were returning home after the Korean War. Martin learned how to lurk around the entrance where sooner or later he would be offered a coca cola by one of the sailors who had come up to the summit on the iconic Peak Tram. The carriage of the tram was divided into a covered, front part and a rear exposed section where there were no walls, restraining ropes or safety bars. Naturally the rear attracted young adventurers like Martin who hung on as the vehicle trundled out from the Garden Road Station, passing the Helena May institute on the lower slopes. From there the gradient became increasingly steep so that at May Road Station it was only possible to alight by holding the bars on the side to steady oneself on the sloping platform. On the way up butterflies and dragon flies droned across the rear and, as one looked back, spectacular views of the city below emerged. Martin comments:

*I grew blasé about the Peak Tram, for I took it as commonly as people might a bus. The view, the harbour a backdrop at the top of the windows, the slopes of the Peak and the buildings apparently leaning backwards at a bizarre angle, were everyday phenomena.*[xxxviii]

On one occasion at the Barker Road Station where there was also a very steep incline and just before the point where the trams going up and down paused at the points, there was a crowd of people on the platform and bright lights blazing. Someone appeared with a clipboard; another called 'Action!' A man appeared in a light suit and boarded the tram. It was Clark Gable. The film being shot was *Soldier of Fortune* with him in the leading role, much to the delight of Joyce who on that occasion was accompanying Martin seated in the open 'coolie' section as the tram descended. Despite her demands and to her great disappointment, Martin refused to chase after the film star for an autograph.

To escape the confines of the Peak Martin took to going down to Western, the oldest part of the colony with its narrow slopping streets and Victorian houses, the verandas crammed with every kind of household god as well as caged birds chirping in chorus. Some of the buildings had spouted bushes from cracks in the walls. Bougainvillaea or jasmine trailed down from pots on the balconies. Dodging coolies negotiating the steps of the ladder streets with their heavy loads, Martin made for the Man Mo Temple dedicated to the Gods of literature (Man) and war (Mo). Man, Cheung wore a green robe while Mo wore a red one. It was said that Mo had been a general in the Han dynasty but, in modern times, was a protector both of policemen and gangsters exemplifying the contradictions that Martin found in Chinese society. Lesser Gods were found in the side altars.

Martin describes the interior vividly:

*Inside, it was sumptuous, rich scarlet banners hanging down with thick, black, dramatic characters upon them. The altar was pristine and the deities most impressive. On the right, just inside the door, sat an old man selling joss-sticks and candles: on the left were a table of lai see packets and some shelves of dusty books. The air was heavy with incense smoke.*[xxxix]

Outside on the narrow ladder streets, he found little cafes and restaurants that specialized in noodles (*won ton*) or served *dim sum* rather than the heartier fare of the *dai pai dongs* of Kowloon or Mongkok. It was a new scene for one who had 'graduated from the Yau Ma Tei School of Street Eating'.[xl]There were also many other stalls and shops, some selling collectors' items like old coins, others more practical things such as keys and knives. The most dazzling was the shop stocking gold which was fashioned in many different forms including Buddha, Ming Warrior or sampans. These different objects were hoarded by the Chinese in case of hard times. The shop was guarded by a burly, turbaned Sikh, armed with a shot gun to deter anyone tempted to break in. In another, suitably gloomy interior, was a carpenter at work on shaping the side of coffin from a plank, curls of reddish wood peeling off his blade. Another man was rounding off the clover leaf end of different coffin, polishing it carefully with sandpaper.

In another street, Martin who admits to never letting any opportunity slip by, looks at the curious jumble of the window display of a shop. Bowls of seeds, bits of dry twig, desiccated bark, dried leaves and roots and shrivelled fungus and flowers are all to be seen. Inside what is a traditional medicine shop was an even odder collection of a mummified tiger's penis and a rhino horn, each item believed to be the cure for a specific ailment. An attendant decided what treatment was needed after duly consulting various sheets of paper and a book. Then he mixed a package, wrapped in paper, for each individual customer. It was another scene from old China.

Sometimes the whole area came alive when a string of firecrackers was released for one celebration or another. Martin observes that:

*The lighting of firecrackers was not restricted to Chinese New Year. Whenever a new shop or business opened, the front of the building was decorated with bamboo scaffolding covered in paper flowers and characters propitiating good fortune. Long strings of firecrackers suspended from roof to pavement would be lit, the street soon filling with choking smoke and the continuous cacophony of explosions. If the building was over five storeys high, they could last an hour.*[xli]

One of the iconic modes of travelling on Hong Kong Island was by tram. The double-decker green cars ran from Kennedy Town in the western district to Shau Kei Wan in the east, with a diversion around the race course at Happy Valley. Martin particularly like riding on the older models which had open upper front and rear seats on the upper decks, providing views of the bustling streets below but also, at eye level, the interiors of buildings that they passed. Noisy and slow, the trams rattled along through the city from the old, battered colonial buildings of Western, through the plush Central District along Des Voeux Road and passed the monumental edifices of the Hong Kong and Shanghai Bank and the Bank of China. Before long the tram reached Wanchai, with its rows of restaurants and sleazy bars, passengers hopping on and off onto small, traffic islands. A less calm incident took place when in a car with his parents, there was a collision with a tram, largely due to Mr Booth veering onto on the tram lines in an attempt to get past. An unpleasant slanging match followed with the irate tram driver until the police arrived to take charge.

The idyllic calm of life on the Peak could be shattered by the typical Hong Kong drama of a typhoon hitting the colony. Living high up in the Mount Austin block was to be in a very exposed position as the winds began to howl around the mountain. The first gusts brought downpours that seeped through the galvanized steel window frames which were supposed to be water proof. While Wong, the energetic houseboy and cook, spent the morning mopping the floor, the signals increased to Number 9, indicating a violent storm. Business in Central closed down, the ferries were berthed in safe havens and residents warned to stay indoors. By then:

*The wind was terrifying. Each gust curved the windows. The building creaked like a galleon under sail. According to the radio, the sustained wind speed was reaching sixty-five miles per hour with gusts at 130. The rain turned squally, lashing the windows. The veranda became an inch-deep pool. In the servants' quarters rain sprayed through the lattice brickwork as if the building were forging ahead through a heavy sea.*[xlii]

As usual the battering lasted a whole day. The next morning was bright and clear: the birds started to sing again and the butterflies fluttered past.

During their time on the Peak, Joyce and Martin continued to visit the staff in the Four Seasons Hotel in Kowloon. Once down in Central they made their way to the Star Ferry Pier where a service ran every fifteen minutes across the harbour to Tsim Sha Tsui. As on the Peak Tram, there was a first – and second – class section, as there still is. Europeans habitually travelled on the enclosed top deck; the lower deck was filled with coolies carrying great poles and baskets containing everything including live animals. *Amahs* squatted in between looking after their wards. As the ferry weaved between ships in the harbour and sampans, a spray would be blown onto the passengers in the lower deck where Joyce chose to travel to see 'how the other half lived'. The ferry's engines could be cut to allow junks to pass in front – one spied by Martin carried a Communist flag. When the ferries berthed there was loud crashing against the side of the piers, constructed of wooden deck on wooden piles which swayed alarmingly. Passengers coming on and off had to hold the hand rails to avoid being thrown off balance.

When not exploring the rich, natural life on the Peak or wandering in the colourful backstreets, Martin did, on occasions, enter the colonial world of British Hong Kong. Tkachenko was Joyce's favourite patisserie (run by White Russian refugees) even though it attracted ladies of leisure, mostly wives of British officials with whom she had little in common. And nearby was the Peninsula Hotel with it famous afternoon teas, another haunt of the expatriate community. However, the most amusing of his encounters with the official world was a visit to Government House itself where Joyce and he were received for a short interview with Sir Alexander Grantham whom, as we have seen, was so helpful to Han Suyin.

The visit had come about because Ah Shun, the family *amah*, had given birth to a child fathered by Wong, the houseboy. When Ken Booth reported this to the naval authorities, the Booths were told that babies were not permitted to live in the servants' quarters at Mount Austin for fear of disturbing the peace of all the residents in the block. Either the child should be sent away to be looked after by relatives or the servants should be dismissed. Joyce was furious and determined to resist. After a further exchange with the authorities, the Booths were told that this was a civil rather than a military matter subject to health and safety regulations. Joyce would not give up despite her husband's opposition. Her stubbornness paid off: finally, an interview with the Governor was granted.

The Governor appeared in a benign mood, shaking hands and asking Martin his name and whether he knew whom he was addressing. The precocious young *gweilo* replied "His Excellency, the Governor, sir."[xliii] The Governor smiled and led them into a comfortable drawing room furnished in the style of an English country house where tea was served. When he explained that it was Chinese tea, Martin told him that he was used to drinking tea in *dai pai dongs.* The Governor joked that Martin was obviously a young China hand, adding laconically "I am afraid, this tea may not be up to the standard of a *dai pai dong.*"[xliv] After a short discussion the audience was brought to a close. As long as the landlord did not object and fire escapes were in order, Ah Shun and the child could continue to live in the servants' quarters. In due course the Governor would propose a change in the regulations which would need to be passed by the Legislative Council. They shook hands again and an elated Joyce rushed out to broadcast her victory for Chinese rights and to tell her friends that Wong's delicious cakes would still be available at her home. This was indeed post-war, colonial Hong Kong.

# Chapter 4
# Diamond Hill: Feng Chi-shun

While Martin Booth was growing up on the verdant and highly protected slopes of the Peak, Feng Chi-shun was being brought up in the much less salubrious area of Diamond Hill on Kowloon's eastern edge. Chi-shun was born in Wuhan, coming to Hong Kong in the nineteen-fifties when his family fled from Communist China along with a flood of refugees from the mainland. They first lived in Shek Kip Mei, a squatter encampment – scene of the serious fire described by Martin Booth in 1952 – before moving to the socially mixed but predominantly poor area of Diamond Hill. A precocious, bright boy encouraged by his father who was a teacher, Chi-sun eventually made it to La Salle College, one of the elite schools in the colony although, according to him, filled with more thuggish types than the debonair boys of the rival Diocesan College. From school, to the great pride of the family he matriculated to Hong Kong university to study medicine in the same faculty headed by Solomon Bard to whom we shall give the last word in this collection.

Feng Chi-shun went onto to study in the United States, became a naturalised American citizen and married an American woman. But once again the lure of Hong Kong called: as a qualified pathologist he returned there to take up a post as an adviser to the Department of Health, by now married for a second time. In later life he took to full-time writing, notably producing fictional work in *Three Wishes in Bardo* which deals with the familiar theme of a displaced Eurasian boy growing up in the turbulent atmosphere of post-war Hong Kong. Like Chi-shun himself his fictional hero heads for America but his life there is not all ease and advancement. However, Chi-shun's most important contribution to a description of Hong Kong during the 1950s and 1960s is *Diamond Hill*, a loosely organised series of autobiographical essays covering his boyhood years in what was for most of its inhabitants a less-favoured area.

The highly atmospheric picture Chi-shun draws of Diamond Hill is set out in a series of topical chapters – family, school, food, gambling and movies. Throughout the narrative dubious characters, con-men and ruffians enliven the scene in 'one of the poorest and most backward villages in Hong Kong when Hong Kong was poor and backward'. [xlv] Chi-shun explains that he looks back to his formative years there with mixed feelings. On the one hand he cherishes memories of a place that was so significant in his youth but on the other hand, he does not want to idealize it by overlooking its harshness. He expresses his relief that the character-building experience of life in that environment came when he was young rather than later in life.

No one seems to know the origin of the district's name though Chi-shun points out that Chinese word suggests a place where stones are excavated. Typically, the buildings were of two stories: shops below and accommodation above. The slopes and lanes of the hill were crammed with shops of every description as well as the typical open food stands for *dan dan* noodles, usually the most affordable item on any menu. Hawkers, selling everything from household goods to cotton clothes, wandered through the streets peddling their wares and jumping aside as traffic fought its way through. Smells of every kind filled the air. The medical practitioner, a former barber, had bottles of snakes and mice, preserved in Chinese wine, on display in his shop window. Small manufacturers were hidden up alleyways producing everything from household goods to statues for decorating altars.

The ethnic divides in Diamond Hill were between the predominantly Guangdong Cantonese, the Chiu Chow refugees and everyone else who, according to Cantonese practice, as we have seen in the case of Han Suyin, were regarded as 'Shanghainese' foreigners wherever they happened to come from in China. Chi-shun's family were partly Chiu Chow. Natives of that region were reputed to be a tough breed, good fighters and very clannish. Chi-shun explains:

*My mother was from Chiu Chow, my father was Shanghainese, and I spoke perfect Cantonese. So, I'd be whatever worked to my advantage, Among Chiu Chow people, I'd be gaa gie noun, I spoke Mandarin with the Shanghainese, and among the Cantonese, no one had to know I was not one of them.*[xlvi]

Even so there were occasions when a dialect, although a version of Cantonese, defeated him.

The ethnic groups formed tribes who looked after their own. There were fights between them and rival gangs within the groups; sometimes the brawls led to violence. Many young men learned Kung Fu as a method of self-defence. One such boy was Chee Kit, a classmate of Chi-shun who acted as his protector in exchange for being able to copy his homework as he was not a good student. The girls also formed gangs and cliques, ready to confer favours on the toughest boys. There were amusing incidents as well as unpleasant ones: Chi-shun and his friends came upon a naked couple cavorting in the bushes only to be shooed away by a posse of bodyguards who were brothers of the man involved. Many of the triad members had been in and out of prison: their confrontation with the police could be violent. Local medicine men did a brisk trade in herbal treatments for bruised and battered bodies.

The Feng family were middle class by local standards, yet seven family members lived in a two-roomed bungalow, with chickens roaming in the backyard. The children did a part-time job making plastic flowers to earn pocket money. Chi-shun had the mischievous energy of a boy of his age roaming the streets with his friends Tai Lin, Ah Bok and Umbrella.

The environment had its rough edge: bus conductors were strong armed men ready to throw anyone off their bus who misbehaved. The buses themselves were double-deckers in their iconic yellow and red paint, with the Kowloon Motor Bus logo emblazoned on the sides. A whole team was involved in running the bus – a driver, a conductor and two fare collectors who went up and down the aisles carrying canvas bags to collect the 10 cents fare from each passenger. Occasionally they were threatened by their passengers and fights ensued. But the crew were also a tough breed; their conversations were littered with foul words. In this hurly burly world Chi-shun soon picked up a spicy repertoire of Cantonese swear words.

The bus route took passengers along Waterloo Road down to central Kowloon. Pupils from different schools stood at the bus stops along the way, ready to jostle their way past any rivals from other schools. No one would give way because that would involve a loss of face. But the penalty for anyone caught misbehaving was expulsion from school so there was a point at which the parties shied away from confronting one another.

At school, despite his father's supervision, Chi-shun did not do well at first. His father had to plead with the headmaster to prevent his son being held back a year in class. Like all Chinese parents, his father was keen for him to do well at school but he did not go to the lengths that one of their neighbours, a Mr Chan. Mr Chan turned up at the headmaster's study to protest when his son had bad results and demanded to review the marking procedures for the exam papers. Everything changed when Chi-shun got into the class of the attractive Miss Yau. All the boys were besotted by her and tried their best to get into her good books. Chi-shun's ruse was to study as hard as possible to gain her approval. However, Miss Yau already had her favourites. One of the boys, Ah Yuk gained the nickname of the 'Grammar King' when he raised questions about English grammar that no one else could understand. Another pupil, Lau Lee-hok, came from a wealthy family who had made their money in the booming garment business. He was a polite, well-behaved boy who jumped out of the family car to walk the last stretch to school so as not to appear too haughty. His charm worked on Miss Yau. The other boys were envious of his being teacher's pet.

The unexpected consequence of Chi-shun's efforts to impress Miss Yau was a sudden improvement in his grades so that soon he was reaching the top end of the class. When the time came, that enabled him to enter La Salle College with his future prospects very much improved. La Salle had a cosmopolitan mix of Portuguese, Chinese, Indian and a few British boys who did not get into King George V, the favoured school for the expatriate community. One of the immediate changes Chi-shun had to adapt to at La Salle was the higher level of English spoken at the school compared to how it was spoken in his primary school. It added to a competitive, one-upmanship atmosphere, each boy trying to prove himself better than anyone else. Chi-shun at first found the atmosphere intimidating and didn't take to the system of prefects which we shall see, Solomon Bard also found an unpleasant feature of the English school he went to in Shanghai. But Chi-shun soon realised that sporting the La Salle tie was a great status symbol in the area, attracting the attention of all the prettiest girls. As he reached the top of the school, he joined an elite band of pupils who were marked out for university education.

At home crammed into a nook near the kitchen was Ah Ho, the family's *amah*. We have seen how significant the role of an *amah* in all Hong Kong family homes. Even though Ah Ho's cooking was rather bland and her cleaning indifferent, Chi-shun's parents were very tolerant of her. That included overlooking her insatiable gambling habit which involved her disappearing each afternoon to play mahjong with her cronies at tables set up in front of shops on the street. On the way home she would shop at the wet market and then cook the evening meal for seven people. Her loyalty to the family was never in doubt: when a taxi was needed, she went down to get it from the village but to save money told the driver not to put the meter on at once. Instead, she would run in front to show him the way to the house; only then telling him to start the meter. Being illiterate, she would enlist Chi-shun's help in writing whatever letters she needed to send to relatives and friends.

Feng senior was himself addicted to gambling 'the curse of the Chinese' [xlvii] arranging all night sessions of mahjong with a habitual gang of friends. Chi-shun knew this was coming when a blanket was laid on the table to blot out the sound of the crashing cubes. Mahjong could also be played publicly, in special parlours, with complete strangers. These were rough places, frequented by ruffians as well as seasoned gamblers. Difficult customers would be dragged out and dealt with by the tough bouncers. All sorts of venues and outlets existed for other forms of gambling from special clubs to modest snooker halls where illegal lotteries – Chi Fa – were run. The gambling dens were run by the triads, they:

*were intimidating places not meant for the faint-hearted. I was not brave enough to mingle with the high rollers, but Umbrella took me there just to watch. There were guards at the entrance and the inside of the establishment was windowless and rustic. The amount of money on the games table was breath-taking.[xlviii]*

Even the billiard parlours could attract petty crimes. The seasoned players would win their games just by a small margin, giving their unsuspecting victims the hope that they might win the next game. Chi-shun was grateful that he was never good enough at snooker to play in the seedy venues scattered around Diamond Hill.

No account of Hong Kong life could leave out the subject of food. In the local cuisine no living creature was excluded: rice worms, water beetles, pig intestines, snakes and frogs were all acceptable ingredients. A meal consisted of *soong* – tasty dishes – added to *bac fan*, white rice which was the staple starch or noodles as a substitute. A large proportion of vegetables in the diet counteracted the probably unhealthy use of cooking lard. Chicken was regarded as a luxury, reserved for special occasions. Preparation began with the slaughtering of the animal in the kitchen, draining the blood from the body and then plucking off the feathers. Once it was cooked, every part was eaten including the feet and bones. Feng Chi-shun's stepmother was a talented cook.

Hailing from Sichuan, she specialised in the hot and spicy dishes of that region: young Chi-shun watched her at work in the kitchen, learning how to cook some of the dishes himself including a favourite winter hotpot braised on charcoal in a special cooking utensil.

Chi-shun confesses to being hungry most of the time since eating at home was confined to mealtimes. Luckily the Cantonese could always be relied upon for providing an endless range of delicious street food at modest cost. An appetising, in-between meals snack was ground beef steamed in a bamboo tray, wrapped around with white, sticky dough. All around the district were *dai pai dongs* or canteens, the haunt of Martin Booth as we have seen. The display of a goat's head was a signal that dogmeat, forbidden by law, was available in the canteen though superstition prevented the consumption of any foreign dogs. Food was served *al fresco* on the streets were customers sat on stools or squatted in the traditional Chinese manner at small, round tables.

In the nearby medicine shops, there were bottles of various herbal concoctions, guaranteed to cure all manner of illness from halitosis to acne and coughing. The use of traditional Chinese medicine was intermingled with practical folklore in treating health problems. Rather than seeking professional advice, it was thought better to rely on the opinion of elders who would have experienced many of the illnesses afflicting younger people. The abiding belief was that illnesses were caused by bad diet so what someone was eating had to be examined and, if necessary, changed so as to help them get better. Different food was the best treatment for various ailments. Western medicine was too expensive for most of the Diamond Hill inhabitants and, in any case, was not entirely trusted. Some practices, like the drinking of the urine of virgin boys, defied any common-sense explanation.

A less salubrious but ubiquitous feature of life in Diamond Hill was drug taking. The centre of the drug scene had always been in the unceded Walled City which remained unregulated and lawless until its demolition in 1994. Opium, heroin and the red pill were the three main kinds of drug; heroin (*paak fan*) the most popular. Addicts inhaled heroin by heating it on foil until a vapour came up which they 'chased' giving the practice the name of 'chasing the dragon'. Another way of taking it was to add a larger amount of white powder so that the vapour rose more quickly. This was known as 'playing the harmonica'. The drug trade was highly organised: the sellers of *paak fan* had stands, known as recharge stations, for their customers. In the Walled City, outside British jurisdiction, the trade in drugs was conducted openly. In Hong Kong proper, things had to be done more discreetly: sometimes the *paak fan* was inserted in cigarettes in place of tobacco and smoked in that way. The smoker kept the cigarette pointing upwards to minimise spillage, a method known as 'firing the missile'.

Chi-shun's visit to the Wall City was conducted by a guide, just as Martin Booth's had been. Mr Chow, a neighbour, had some connections there and he took them through the narrow, almost hidden entrance into the maze of lanes where only bicycles could comfortably navigate. Chi-shun tells us that the entire Walled City was not a sin city: it was divided into districts. The western part housed people who had regular, outside connections including a daily commute to work. There were also small manufacturing businesses within that area. The eastern side, on the other hand, was more enclosed with narrow, dark alleyways instead of open streets. It became lit up at night by the candlelight of addicts cooking their heroin. As well as drugs there was a variety of pornographic entertainment, enacted for the most part by drug addicts. Chi-shun and his adolescent companions found these entertainments freakish rather than erotic as they had hoped.

A less sinister side of Diamond Hill was its unexpected link to the film world. Movie production in Hong Kong had expanded greatly in the late 1950s; films were made in Cantonese, Mandarin and English and the studios were located in Diamond Hill. Some of the studios were fairly basic:

*There were trees and gardens and low-rise office buildings around but the inside of the studio itself looked like a barn – spacious, rustic, with a tall ceiling and a dirt floor. There were electric wires all over the place and it seemed the most important thing was lighting. A lot of people spent a lot of time in arranging the lights.* [xlix]

When a tea lady appeared with a tray of fruits, everyone working on the sets dropped whatever they were doing and production temporarily stopped. Among the crew the most highly respected were the camera men since the actors knew that a slight tilt or variation of the shot being taken, they would appear in a better or worse light. If Chi-shun was challenged by anyone to explain his presence in a studio, he claimed to be a relative of Louis Cha, Kung Fu writer and movie maker. Of the films produced the Cantonese ones were considered low brow and vulgar, sometimes mixing opera scores with Kung Fu scenes. The Mandarin productions were more sophisticated and the first to be made in colour. Much of the investment in the business had been made by Run Run Shaw, an entrepreneur who had come from Shanghai among the stream of immigrants in the 1950s. He would sometimes frequent one of the local restaurants, his presence easily known by a gleaming car parked outside. The films he supported became box office successes.

Western films also had considerable success: Clark Gable, whose autograph we have seen Joyce Booth had been keen to get, featured in *Soldier of Fortune* while *A Many Splendoured Thing*, based on Han Su Yin's novel starring William Holden and Jennifer Jones as Han Suyin herself. The screen version of Richard Mason's *Suzie Wong* became the most famous film of all with Nancy Kwan, a local actress in the leading role. When students keen on improving their English were not watching these movies, they were listening to Pat Boone or Elvis Presley. Their elders preferred Frank Sinatra, Bing Crosby and Nat King Cole.

Although films in English were popular, Chi-shun recalls that the language was not well spoken by the majority:

*The standard of English in those days, in my opinion, was not as high as today in spite of all the complaints we hear from many quarters to the contrary. There were far fewer English speakers then, but those who were proficient might have been better than today's average English speakers. You didn't see or hear as horrendously bad English as often as today because those who didn't know English well would not write it publicly and would keep their mouths shut.[1]*

There was a particular difficulty in pronouncing 'v' and 'sh' so that pop groups' names were distorted by their young fans: the 'Ventures' became the 'Wentures' the 'Shadows' the 'Saddles'. After all, Cantonese was the *lingua franca*.

If life for the poor folk of Diamond Hill could be hard, it was not without fun. An adventurous spirit permeates Chi-shun's writing which is confident and upbeat in tone. He is of course writing about his years as a lively teenager, roaming around the area with his adventurous friends. Nevertheless, he says that there wasn't really a community spirit in Diamond Hill because the majority of its inhabitants were refugees who, if they were successful, moved on to live in other parts of the colony. One of the Feng's neighbours was in the garment business: as soon as his business flourished, he moved off to Hong Kong Island without even saying a word of farewell. When another friend's mother inherited some money, they cleared off to North Point. Others, like his friend Tai Lin, worked hard and lived frugally so that they could save the deposit for a tiny apartment elsewhere in Kowloon. Some even went abroad to establish restaurant businesses. The Fengs themselves moved to Ho Man Tin as soon as his father found a better paid job.

Nevertheless, in his gang of boys there was plenty of fun to be had without spending much money. They used 10 cents coins to play dice. Simple games could be played for nothing just using bottle caps which would be aimed at a row as if in skittles with whoever could knock down the most, winning the round. The caps could also be flattened and pierced, then threaded and used as weapons. A favourite pastime was kite flying. The thread on which the kite was attached could be sharpened with an oil mix containing crushed glass and used to cut down opponents' threads. Chi-shun records his pride at being most successful among his friends in cutting down others' kites. Other games could involve cruelty to insects: crickets were pitched against each other to fight. On the other hand, fireflies were collected because they shone out, giving free lighting reminding Chi-shun of an ancient fable in which a boy too poor to buy oil, collected fireflies in a transparent bag so that he could study at night. Eventually the young man's diligence enabled him to pass the national examination to enter the civil service and he became a much-respected mandarin.

One local green space was the gardens of the Chi Lin nunnery which could be entered free of charge. It was a place of peace and quiet. One could even indulge in reading in its shady corners, finding treasure as the old Chinese saying went, in a book. Chi-shun complains that later when the nunnery had become a tourist attraction, it had completely lost its old-world charm. Sometimes he would take his family dog, Mabel, for a walk in its grounds. When the dog died, Chi-shun stuffed its body into an old hemp sack which had previously been used to store rice. Putting the sack into a trolley he pushed it along Mabel's favourite route, crossing a bridge, then some new apartment blocks until they reached the open hills. He and Ah Fai dug a hole and buried the body in the pouring rain. He told his younger companion that the rain is a sign that the sky is mourning for Mabel. He was secretly grateful that the rain disguised the tears running down his cheeks.

There were also more respectable outings with the family such as attending church on Sundays. For the most part sermons were delivered in Mandarin but when a Western pastor appeared, they were given in English much to the delight of those who prided themselves on their English proficiency. Chi-shun was never devout and felt the urge to keep the few coins his stepmother gave him instead of putting them in the collection bag. Among his friends, some of the conversions to Christianity were entirely opportunistic. Tai Lin's mother, who worshipped various Buddhist Gods, makes a sudden conversion when she discovers that the Catholic Church is distributing free food. She has the whole family baptised speedily. However, when it comes to the clothes the Church gives out, some of the family members will not wear them as being seen in worn-out handouts would be a huge loss of face.

In *Diamond Hill* Chi-shun captures the vibrant atmosphere of a street-level Hong Kong where so much life – whether for food, gambling or just sitting about – is done out of doors, usually in a crowded environment on pavements or in the throughfares themselves. It is a life far removed from the luxury and glamour of the clubs and hotel lobbies frequented by the expatriate and rich Chinese communities we have seen but it is the Hong Kong where the vast majority of its people eke out a living and where they socialise and enjoy what pleasures they can, particularly in having communal meals together.

It is also a corrupt society in which the police cannot be relied upon. Chi-shun and his friends see the uniformed police doing their daily rounds, collecting protection money while helping themselves to the produce of stall owners. The plain clothes branch is even worse, their behaviour hardly distinguishing them from the triads. He describes a typical scene:

*We watched a policeman trying to chase down a thug, and dramatically the hat fell off his head, and that stopped the policeman in his tracks, because he had to pick up the hat and look for clues inside. Some older guy told us, in a conspiratorial tone, that there would be a hundred-dollar bill tucked inside.*[li]

His description of life in Diamond Hill is the backdrop of post-war Hong Kong where refugees, like the Feng family, join the stream of a fast developing, urban environment unrivalled anywhere else in the Far East. Many of the newcomers had to adapt to urban conditions to which they were not accustomed but they maintained their traditional family life and practices. In Diamond Hill the food stalls, hawkers and dens of vice are all jumbled together; every type of personality from *amahs* to gangsters inhabit its streets and alleyways. It is a colourful, noisy scene which disguises what can be lives of hardship, though not as extreme as some of the rural areas of China from which the refugees have come. Chi-shun laments its passing and replacement by anonymous looking tower blocks with a gleaming MTR station and shopping mall at its centre.

Diamond Hill in the 1950s and 1960s was a tough place and, as Chi-shun shows us, was not a place for the faint-hearted, teaching its youngsters how to survive in a world far removed from the protective recesses of colonial Hong Kong.

# Chapter 5
# The World of Suzie Wong: Richard Mason

Richard Mason was an exact contemporary of Austin Coates, born just after the First World War and like Coates, lived to the end of the twentieth century. They shared a similar experience of war-time service in the Royal Air Force (both doing intelligence work) which led to assignments abroad, in Mason's case in Burma. As a result, like Coates, he became an intrepid traveller who eventually made it to distant Polynesia: his novels reflect his globe-trotting life. In his early days Mason was influenced by W. H. Auden who happened to be a teacher at Downs Malvern School where the young Richard was educated. Precocious and no doubt encouraged by Auden, Mason already wrote a novel as a schoolboy which, however, his mentor criticized on the grounds that the characters in the story fell in love too quickly. It was a lesson that Richard did not forget as we shall see in his treatment of the love story of Suzie Wong.

Richard continued writing right throughout his school days, turning out articles for the local press and for a film magazine. His wartime experience included learning Japanese so as to be able to carry out interrogation of prisoners for intelligence purposes. That background is captured in his second novel, *The Wind Cannot Read* (1947) where the hero of the story learns Japanese while living in the unlikely venue of a flat overlooking the harbour of Bombay. After the war literary success enabled Mason to travel extensively including a heroic trip driving through Africa in a second-hand car. He later retired to Rome where he took up sculpting and confessed to enjoying a more sedate and comfortable life with his third wife.

Mason's wartime experience coloured his first novel, *The Body Fell on Berlin* as well as *The Wind Cannot Read.* He subsequently wrote the screenplay for a version of the latter novel starring Dirk Bogarde, coming to the height of his acting career, in 1958. By the time of the film Mason had already won the

John Llewellyn prize and had become an established writer both of novels and film scripts, used to adapting the settings of plots to different media. What remained constant was his pursuit of love stories, particularly involving characters who come from different cultures. Following that theme he decided, somewhat impetuously, to visit Hong Kong in 1956 seeking inspiration from a new setting. During a short visit of a few months, he dashed off the first version of *The World of Suzie Wong* which, however, was only published a year later in a largely revised form.

Determined to immerse himself in local rather than ex-patriate culture in Hong Kong, Mason checked into the Luk Kwok Hotel near the Mission to Seamen in Wanchai. At the time Wanchai was not a district in which any European would be living: Mason observes that a minute's stroll from the centre and one would not even see a European face let alone find a foreigner in residence. That is exactly what he was looking for in Wanchai with 'its teeming alleyways with litter filled gutters, and pavement vendors, the street stalls, the excitement and bustle'.[lii] The district was authentically Chinese, entirely local and was a thousand miles away in spirit from the colonial setting of the Peak.

The Luk Kwok Hotel turned out to be a brothel which Mason used in his novel, renaming it the Nam Kwok. His fictional hotel served the same purpose as the actual establishment which was to entertain seamen who had come ashore from the numerous visiting ships, both British and American. Situated on the waterfront it was surrounded by other similar establishments in what was a well-known red-light district. Any expatriate seen in the area could only be looking for an illicit rendezvous.

Mason filled the Nam Kwok with a community of girls, mostly Cantonese but with the odd refugee from Shanghai and the statutory Eurasian, all speaking different versions of Chinese as well as different standards of English. Thrown together in a band, the girls have their own code of honour which includes keeping out of one another's engagement with a chosen, regular customer. If he was Chinese, he would probably be a married man seeking solace outside the confines of an arranged marriage. No one thought anything unusual about that. The ladies are polite and well-mannered; they are also very good judges of character no doubt helped by dealing with every kind of individual who comes through the doors of the hotel. Mason's portrayal of the Nam Kwok ladies is highly sympathetic and given the times, highly unconventional. To the

Europeans the girls were outcasts; to the Chinese merely performing a time-honoured role as concubines, however sleazy the setting they were in.

The hero of the novel is Robert Lomax, an artist who has taken up permanent residence in the Nam Kwok. His studio has a balcony which gives him a panoramic view of the harbour. At night it was spectacularly lit up and crowded with ships and boats of every description including the iconic junks. The area was also famous for its street food which was cheap and could be ordered in at any hour of day or night. Robert would have his meals on the balcony watching the lights in the harbour in front of him. Earlier in the evening he would saunter down to the hotel lobby where the girls sit around waiting for customers. They look upon him as a sort of protector, a shield from their predatory customers. The atmosphere there is set by the playing of 'Seven Lonely Hearts' on the juke box. Among the girls, whom Lomax considers to be good girls despite their profession, is Suzie Wong (Wong Mee Ling), one of the liveliest. Despite a lack of sexual contact between Robert and herself, she considers that he is her property, coming up frequently to his room to admire his art work and in time to become a subject of his portrait painting.

Bearing all the feminine charms of an Oriental woman, Suzie is a character of considerable courage and a real survivor. The most important principle guiding her life is the very Chinese value of self-respect; any suggestion that she is not actually Robert's mistress would be a great loss of face, something well understood by all her companions who behave as if she was. And being a mistress was a perfectly acceptable position to hold in the Chinese family context. Gradually her emotional attachment to Robert becomes real despite the lack of any physical expression of her affection. She exudes an air of confidence in claiming his attentions but in fact comes more and more to rely on his calm and welcoming presence.

Among her companions all this is a source of great esteem fanning the notion of romantic love they still harbour despite the outward sordidness of their profession. Although debarred from good marriages because they have lost their virginity, the Nam Kwok girls display something of the practical Chinese attitude to sex which is a tradable commodity but does not affect the soul. Although there are occasional squabbles between them, the girls are members of a sisterhood in which each person is supported by the others.

Several episodes occur during the gradual build-up of the love affair between Suzie and Robert monitored by Ah Tong, one of the band of influential houseboys who manages the floor of the hotel where Robert's room is located. The first is Suzie's affair with Ben Jeffcoat, a married man of 35 who moves seamlessly between the world of the Kit Kat Club in Central and the Nam Kwok. He is a successful entrepreneur with a large house on the Peak but is bored with his marriage to Elizabeth, his obsessive and demanding wife. The affair with Suzie coming at a time when Ben's 'features show signs of coarsening too early and running to seed',[liii] rejuvenates him. He becomes entirely obsessed with her, calling by each day to be with her. When she breaks their exclusive relationship by having a fling with a young sailor, Ben storms into the Nam Kwok to give her a sound trashing. This is seen by Suzie and the other girls as a great triumph since it shows Ben's jealous commitment to her. Nevertheless, as Robert Lomax realises the affair will not last: in due course Ben returns to the nest of his married home and Suzie is abandoned. Reflecting on the affair she concludes that Ben is emotionally incapable of loving anyone at all including his wife. Suzie feels no bitterness towards her: as another woman in Ben's life, she is equally a victim.

No sooner has Ben disappeared from the scene when an even more bizarre suitor in the person of Rodney Tessler appears at the Nam Kwok to claim Suzie. Rodney is a wealthy but mercurial young American who rides around the colony in a shining Buick. He has family connections to an art gallery in New York which he suggests can be an outlet to sell Robert's works. Rodney soon becomes another obsessive client of Suzie's moving out of the Gloucester Hotel and into the Nam Kwok so as to be near her. His room is also on Ah Tong's floor but the houseboy does not approve of him, regarding him as an intruder who is getting in the way of his 'regulars'. Whenever Suzie comes upstairs to visit Robert, Rodney emerges from his nearby room and joins them, claiming that he must keep company with his 'Goddess'. A melodramatic scene frequently followed:

*He claimed to be struck dumb at the sight of Suzie's beauty, and fell to his knees at her feet – a pantomime that by now had become a familiar accompaniment to his entrance.*[liv]

Suzie's persistent refusal to have sex with him drives him into rages calling her a nasty sailor's whore and turning his ire on Robert as well. After a flaming row in the Nam Kwok peace is restored to the point where Suzie and Robert agree to an excursion in Rodney's gleaming Buick. As they drive through Central, Rodney's black mood returns fuelled by jealousy as his two guests chat happily in the back seat. He orders the chauffeur to stop the car; jumps out telling the driver to take the pair wherever they wish to go. Robert is alarmed wondering if Rodney is in a suicidal mood but Suzie assures him that he is not. Robert reflects on his partner's intuition:

*This sixth sense of Suzie's, like the sharpened sense of smell that counterbalances blindness, counterbalanced her illiteracy. It often afforded her astonishing flashes of insight; and although these flashes occurred unpredictably, and never to order, whenever they did occur, they proved unerring, and I came to place in them an explicit trust.*[lv]

Without more ado the couple abandon the car, make their way up a bustling street into a warren of concrete buildings to find the lair of a fortune teller whom Suzie wants to visit to find out what is in store for her. He is a clean-shaven, monk-like character who makes great play of consulting charts and almanacs and delights his client with a prediction that she will visit England.

The episode with Rodney had not yet reached a conclusion. Recovering his confidence, he invites Suzie to live with him as his mistress but his overpowering possessiveness dooms the relationship to last for less than a week. As a last attempt to lure her for good, Rodney proposes a holiday in Thailand but on the day of departure, Suzie does not show up. Instead, Robert pursues Rodney to the airport to find out what has happened as Suzie has disappeared from the Nam Kwok. She has left thinking that Robert's own one night stand with Betty Lau is the beginning of a serious affair between them.

Suzie finds work in a bar in Kowloon but Robert tracks her down in her hideout where she has fled to avoid recognition. He brings her back to the Nam Kwok: their affair now begins in earnest. Curiously there is an innocence about it; Suzie can only undress in the dark and bursts into tears at its consummation. The couple also manage a trip by ferry to Macau. There they enjoy the peace and quiet of the sleepy town and their anonymity.

During the period when the love affair between Robert and Suzie grows – and this takes time so it seems that Mason has taken on board Auden's dictum that love cannot come too soon – Suzie is bringing up a child that she has borne from an itinerant, American father who has disappeared. She is devoted to the infant who is looked after by an *amah* in the cubicle that Suzie rents nearby, using up all her hard-earned income at the Nam Kwok. Whenever she can, she leaves the hotel to visit her child and sometimes takes Robert along with her. A devastating episode in the story is when the child is killed in a fire which sweeps through the building leaving Suzie heart-broken and sapped of all energy. Accompanied by Robert to the rubble that was once her home she is unconcerned about searching for a tin with her savings in it. When a security guard cannot find it:

*She shrugged indifferently: the loss of the money meant nothing to her beside the loss of the baby and it had [not] occurred to her that she had lost everything she possessed in the world except the soaked clothes she was wearing.*[lvi]

Mason's story is graphically set in Hong Kong of the 1950s, in the same era of Austin Coates and Han Suyin. It soon became a bestseller: when Roman Rodamilans, Austin's Spanish friend and correspondent, finds it in a bookstore in California, he is thrilled calling it his favourite novel set in Hong Kong. Mason is particularly good at evoking the atmosphere of the colony's backstreets, crammed and chaotic as they were. Clambering through the maze Robert records:

*We reached an intersecting road and turned off trough a vegetable market, and past an open site that at first glance appeared to be a rubbish dump, and at second glance a gigantic rabbit-warren because of the holes in the rubbish like burrows and at third glance, a human-warren, which is what it was – a colony of squatters' huts made from old sacking, rotting wood and flattened-out tins.*[lvii]

In the crowded streets around the Nam Kwok Robert gets used to buying lychees from the bunches that hang at the entrance to a shop, avoiding washing that has fluttered down from the bamboo poles on which it was drying. The sound of crashing mahjong tiles coming out of the open windows fills the air. Another preoccupation is with food: there are open-air stands on every corner selling noodles and other local delicacies. Vegetables brought in from the New Territories and the mainland are stacked in wicker baskets along arcades where men wearing singlets sit on the pavements watching the world go by.

Loud conversations, which sound as if people are shouting at each other, come out of the open doors of tea houses. There is nothing reserved about the Cantonese at play; they are positively Gallic in their vivacity. In nearby canteens, others are gobbling tray after tray of dim sum brought around by waitresses screaming out what each basket contains. At night homeless people shelter in the arcades, their possessions flung about around them so that they can avoid any downpour of rain.

Now and again colonial elements are woven into the scenes. On one occasion the lovers go to the race course at Happy Valley. Surrounded by squatters' huts on the nearby hills, the gambling-addicted punters cheer on their favourite jockey and horse. When the:

*first race had finished women in black trousers and wide conical straw hats were spread out in a line across the track, pressing down loosened turf with their bare feet. A bass band with uniformed Chinese bandsmen playing 'Poet and Peasant'.*[lviii]

In the meantime, everyone invades the bar for a drink: rich Chinese gentlemen in high-necked gowns or well-tailored suits, their wives in dazzling *cheong-sams* and trailed by a whiff of Parisian perfume were mixed with colonial officers in white jackets or military uniform. Drinks are brought into the special boxes reserved for businessmen from the top corporations in the colony. There is an air of pampered privilege at every turn; the betting and gambling reach proportions that would support ordinary families for weeks.

Robert sometimes leaves his bohemian existence in Wanchai to join a friends' party on the Peak. Taking the Peak tram up to May Road, he reaches the Hamiltons' spacious flat for cocktails, followed by a formal dinner. Drinks are served by sleek houseboys who move about silently, bearing silver trays. The guests are dressed to the nines: stiff jackets for the men; silk dresses for the ladies. Silver glistens on the sideboards. Robert is reminded of the gossipy colonial world that has been so familiar to him in the past. Complaints about servants, the natives and lack of certain facilities is the staple of these conversations with some occasional malicious gossip thrown in.

A nasty tone enters the dinner table chatter when one of the 'Old China hands' cautions against being kind to Eurasians which only has the effect of making them feel above their station, thinking they are as good as those who are being pleasant to them. There is a smug air of superiority leading Robert to conclude:

*And this lack of charity for fellow human beings – for a minority of unhappy, raceless people fathered by ourselves – seemed to me an incomparably worse sin than any to be found at the Nam Kwok; and my respect and affection for the Nam Kwok girls, who in the main were incapable of such intolerance and inhumanity, came back to me in an overwhelming flood.*[lix]

Robert has become entirely converted to the world of Suzie Wong.

# Chapter 6
# Kampoon Street: Lin Tai-yi

Lin Tai-yi's family background was intensely literary. Her father, Lin Yu Tang was a well-known novelist, translator and philosopher. His works, written in a flowing style, were well known abroad and introduced many Western readers to Chinese culture. In one of his creative moments, he sketches a dialogue between the legendary sage of Taoism, Lao-Tze and Confucius who were contemporaries. This classical, intellectual background had a considerable influence on Lin Tai-yi, born in 1936, as we have seen it did for Han Suyin. At the age of thirteen, she wrote an account of her family with her sister, Adet Lin, who also became a writer. By that time the family had moved to the US where Lin Tai-yi went to school, eventually graduating from Columbia University. Subsequently she taught Chinese at Yale for a short period. But fate destined a return to the East: she married R. Ming Lai, a civil servant working for the Hong Kong Government. The couple took up residence in the colony where Lin Tai-yi became an editor of *Readers Digest*, maintaining the role for several decades. She also wrote in various newspapers and journals. In 1988 she and her family returned to the US.

By the time Kampoon Street was published in 1964 she had already written a number of other novels as well as producing full-length translations of Chinese classics, some in collaboration with her sister. Her early works dealt with the horrors of the Sino-Japanese war and its effects on ordinary people. *War Tide* (1943) was the first of these patriotic novels depicting the harshness of life in China during this period. In *The Golden Coin* (1946) an illiterate woman, Sha, is at the centre of the narrative. Her life is entirely dominated by circumstances so she feels she has no right to speak about spontaneous emotions like love. Her escape was to marry a teacher but one whose lifestyle had little connection to her own, deprived background.

A number of Lin Tai-yi's novels crossed the China/US divide; she returned to an historical background in *The Lilacs Overgrow* (1960) set at the time of the emergence of the People's Republic. The story tells of the trials and tribulations of the wealthy, liberal Wong family (reflecting the author's own family) whose son, Zan is studying in the US while the family is based in Shanghai. The Wongs have to flee as the Communists gain control in northern China among throngs of panic-stricken refugees. Their story is a highly charged, emotional drama. Despite this turbulent background Lin Tai-yi, like Han Suyin, remains a Chinese patriot at heart. For much of her life she was cut off from her Chinese roots but nevertheless expresses her love of China by saying:

*I wish I could hold China, feel it, see the whole of it.*[ix]

*Kampoon Street* stands out in the canon of Hong Kong writing because, apart from a brief connection with the glitzy world of colonial society through the character of the playboy Sunny and his family, the story is largely set in the poorer slums. Nor do any Europeans figure in the narrative. Lin Tai-yi tells us that the street, as well as the characters in the story, is fictional but with its closed in verandas, cubicles and bamboo poles of washing across the street, it could be anywhere in the Yau Ma Tei or Mongkok of the period or even in the backstreets of Suzie Wong's Wanchai. The principal character in the novel is Eling, an ageing, soon-to-become widow, who struggles to maintain her dignity and the welfare of her children, Riri an attractive young lady and Lam, a precocious schoolboy. Eling is a survivor in the rough and tumble of poorer Hong Kong.

The story begins with the death of Ati, the children's father. There is a suggestion that Eling has contributed to his death by not paying enough attention to his ailing condition dismissing it as serious flu, when, in fact, it is deadly pneumonia. The medical aides who arrive tell her that Ati should have had medical treatment long before and may have survived if he had had it. Eling seems genuinely shocked. Although feeling guilty, she nevertheless refuses to spend more than the bare minimum of her savings on Ati's funeral, defying traditional custom which entails an elaborate ceremony at considerable cost. All her efforts have been to save enough money for Lam to attend school and, by getting a better job as a qualified person when he has graduated, lifting them all out of poverty. The reader does not feel the urge to condemn her: it seems that

Ati contributed little to the struggle which she has had to keep the family from sinking into the mire which surrounds them in Kampoon Street.

The family lives in an extremely restricted space on the first floor of a rickety, old building. Their accommodation is no more than a couple of cubicles with bunks and a veranda space where either Riri or Lam escapes to sleep. The neighbours are crowded around them: one of the closest on the next veranda is Duck Face, a barber who has designs on Riri though she does not share his feelings. Lam detests Duck Face. Their daily exchange of insults eventually reaches a point of fury when both fight each other fiercely, causing considerable injuries to themselves before the neighbours rush in to separate the blood-drenched pair.

Most of the relations with neighbours are supportive. One of them, Sookmo, is particularly helpful, looking after Eling when her husband passes away and feeding the children. The most prosperous person in the community is Awabi who runs an outlet store. She persuades Eling that she could make a good living out of selling a special rice wine if she can increase the quantity she makes significantly. Customers will order dozens rather than a few bottles if they are available. Awabi has contacts and will only keep a modest commission for herself. She tells Eling that it is much more realistic to concentrate on building up a business rather than saving every penny to pay for Lam's school fees in the hopes that in future he will land a good job. It would be better if he went out to work straightaway.

The rice wine, which they make at home, is a Hakka type in which water and wine were mixed:

*The bottles gave off a coral light, and the air was soon filled with the wine's heady scent, which triumphed over the smell of human beings collected together in the heat of the floor. [Eling] tamped the corks down and took the bottles away, turning them upside down to mix the water and wine, and put them in the cases in which they had come. Then there was only the sunlight shining harshly into the cubicle as before.*[lxi]

Despite their meagre capital and the cramped quarters in which they live, Eling decides to follow Awabi's advice. They need to buy a large cask which can be stored in Ati's empty cubicle; other equipment and a good supply of water will also be needed. There is no alternative but to spend the money she has put aside for Lam's fees: he must give up schooling for a month.

When the family themselves try to sell the wine from door to door in Prince Edward Road, they are turned away because the people living there prefer Western products rather than local, Chinese ones. One of the inhabitants in a block of flats, an elegantly turned-out lady, is surprised on hearing the vendors speaking fluently. Eling indignantly explains that she and the family are educated people; her husband was a type setter, Lam attends a grammar school. After they have left, she realises that their appearance, in old clothes, does not inspire confidence in potential customers. Lam should have worn his school uniform to impress people.

They manage to sell some wine through Awabi. But wanting to increase sales, Eling and Riri discover that a good location to sell the wine is outside the main hospital. Trade becomes brisk. Lam can go to school, which he loves, with a clear conscience. However, the good luck does not last: mother and daughter are nearly arrested by a policeman for peddling the wine in a public place without a licence. He lets them off after confiscating a few bottles for himself. The loss of income forces Lam to ask the school principal to see if he can get a month's credit for fees.

Even so important customs are not set aside. The family make an outing to the cemetery to propitiate Ati's spirits in the traditional Chinese manner. The cemetery was built on the side of a hill, some distance from the nearest train station in the New Territories.

*There were quite a few people upon the hill, families standing in clusters of black or white, and piles of food set out before some graves. Incense was smoking and all kinds of paper furniture was being burned, so that the dead would have all the comforts of this earth in the other world.*[lxii]

Lam was not convinced that the spirits of the dead really haunted the earth until they were propitiated but on the other hand, it was an insurance policy to attend to them just in case. Eling had made sure that they had brought food with them which, after offering to the dead, she repacked for the family picnic in the nearby field. As the family eat their meal, a blue jay flies over them, something that Eling regards as a good omen. Her mood becomes buoyant. Lam relaxes and links his arm around his mother's but Riri remains determinately independent.

As they leave the hillside, Eling spots some wild watercress growing in the mud and plucks it up to take home.

When the family get back to Kampoon Street, Duck Face rushes out to tell them that he has found a job for Riri working in the beauty salon of the Paradise Hotel, a typical Hong Kong venue for the wealthy. They must rush there at once before the job is taken up by someone else. Hardly have mother and daughter caught breath, when they find themselves on the Star Ferry crossing over to Central where the hotel is located.

As they approach it Riri sees that:

*The Paradise Hotel was taller and wider than the buildings beside it, and the main entrance was brightly lighted. Behind the glass door she saw a very large lobby, with a thick carpet and a fountain in the center and a bank of elevators at the rear. To one side of the door there were sofas and armchairs, where people sat sipping drinks. Bell-boys dressed in black satin jackets and trousers were opening the doors for the guests.*[lxiii]

Chandeliers, lilac-coloured walls and glistening mirrors decorate the beauty salon. After a brief exchange and a white lie on Riri's part (she pretends she has worked in a beauty salon before) she is taken on by Old Chew, its owner, who shows an unhealthy interest in her physique. She is confined to simple tasks at first but soon finds herself manicuring the hands of a Mrs Tung, a lady dressed in the most expensive foreign clothes and whose fingers are covered by enormous diamond rings which have to be removed for the treatment. When Riri tells Mrs Tung about her mother's wine making, Mrs Tung says that her Hakka daughter-in-law who is expecting a child would be interested in trying it.

The Tungs are an extremely wealthy family who have made their fortune from construction during the post-war building boom in Hong Kong. They live in a mansion in Repulse Bay, well away from the bustle of the city. The rooms of the house are furnished in a lavish style, with lacquered furniture, brocaded chairs and Tientsin carpets. Mrs Tung tells Riri to have some wine delivered to their home so that the family can sample it. When Riri tells Eling this news, the old lady and Lam set off on the journey from Kampoon Street laden with wine. It is a long journey, first getting to the Star Ferry pier, crossing the harbour and then taking a long bus ride over the hills to the south side of the island, laden with their caskets. The world they encounter is a very different one from Kampoon Street. As they ride over the hill:

*There came into sight, great isolated houses – villas with smooth white surfaces, pink stucco bungalows embedded in the hearts of private gardens, and Spanish style castles! There was no flat land, but gardens, tier after tier, were carved out from the sides of the hills.* [lxiv]

At the nearby beach there are half-naked people sprawled out in the sand, enjoying the sun. There is a holiday atmosphere far removed from the daily grinding toil of the Tsoi family and their neighbours. Finding the Tung's house but getting no answer when they ring the bell, rather gingerly they push the gate open and enter the grounds. It proves to be a disastrous move as two huge dogs rush out and attack Eling, knocking her over and biting her. Lam shrieks out for help; an unhelpful, old housekeeper shouts out that peddlers are not admitted. But when he realises the seriousness of the situation, an ambulance is called. Eling is rushed off to hospital where she is sedated and put into a general ward. There she must stay until tests are made on the dogs in case they might be rabid.

However, despite this harrowing incident, the connection with the Tung family does not end. When Riri and Lam return to the Repulse Bay house to collect the wine that has been left there, a young man in a flashy sports car comes speeding into the gates opened once more by the grumpy caretaker who tries to keep Riri and Lam out. The 'Young Master' is Sunny Tung who when told of what happened, immediately pays up for the broken bottles of wine, eyeing Riri up and down as he hands her the notes. Riri is not in the mood to be stopped: she forces Lam to go with her to the nearby beach, sensing that that is where Sunny is headed as well. Brother and sister change into hired swimsuits but before they can reach the water, Riri spies Sunny sitting on a deck with a plain looking Hakka woman. She parades herself in front of him, a message he does not fail to understand. He rushes after the pair as they leave, offering them a lift to the Star Ferry and throwing in an invitation for a Saturday night rendezvous with Riri.

Sunny, the playboy, prides himself on being a connoisseur of women but he is in fact besotted by Riri. When they do go out, he takes her to a hidden, dimly lit dance hall:

*They did not talk. They sat mutely, holding hands. She felt his breath close to her cheek, and his eyes upon her, although she could not see him.*[lxv]

Before long he drags her off to a private room where they become lovers, Riri surprised at the depth of her own desire. Sunny is elated at his conquest and determined to show Riri off to his friends. He tells her to buy herself some decent clothes to boost her image. When Eling learns of this development, she is entirely pragmatic calculating that this affair may change the family fortune. She discharges herself from hospital and takes her daughter to a shop selling fine, silk material so that a dress can be made for her. Sunny's friends are duly impressed by the glamorous Riri whom he parades like a trophy on an evening out in the night clubs.

Sunny takes on Riri as his mistress. Eling understands this at once and is complicit in encouraging Riri in the relationship. The family fortunes change: Sunny allocates an apartment in one of the blocks the family own and soon Eling, Lam and Riri have moved out of Kampoon Street into a flat of unimaginable comfort with a kitchen of their own and a proper bathroom. Lam returns to school telling the headmaster that his sister has got a job so that he can make up for the previous unpaid fees.

While Eling does everything to humour Sunny, conscious that they are now financially dependent on him, Lam does not like his sister's suitor at all, even more so when he sees that she has fallen in love with him. His premonition of something bad proves to be right: when Riri becomes pregnant and decides to keep the child to be, Sunny disengages himself from the Tsoi family, withdrawing not only Riri's allowance but throwing them out of the flat. The family are forced to return to Kampoon Street. Although obviously disappointed, Eling's maternal instincts triumph: not only is she supportive of Riri and her grandchild to be but on a visit to the mansion, she tells Mrs Tung that she too will be a grandmother. That does not go down well with the *grande dame*. She shrieks out in front of the astonished *amahs*:

*Curse you, Eling! You will not live very long! Curse you and your son and daughter and unborn child! You deserve to die! There will be no one to mourn you when you die!*[lxvi]

Eling, shocked, leaves the house at once. But she is stoical about the reversal of their fortune. And things change again when Riri is promoted to being a hostess, named Golden Mist, at the Paradise Hotel with prospects of a good income.

The twists and turns of Lin Tai-yi's story are set against a graphic backdrop of the less salubrious backstreets of Hong Kong where most of the population lives. While we see the familiar sights – of the bustling harbour from the Star Ferry, the leisurely beauty of Repulse Bay and the glitzy interior of establishments like the Paradise Hotel, the focus of the novel is on Kampoon Street. It is a typical local scene of small traders as Lam describes:

*He picked his way carefully, stepping over sleeping forms and around pots of rice bubbling on charcoal stoves… he saw the lamp-shade maker bending his wires in front of his shop, and the carpenter and coal merchant could each be dimly made out in the dark recesses of their shops. And there was his uncle Ah Sook squatting in front of his doorway shop, eating his supper like a sparrow picking food from the ground.[lxvii]*

Dark staircases lead into the houses, with bamboo poles hanging washing across the verandas. Here in tiny, cramped cubicles with unpleasant smells rising from the garbage littered street, the family eke out a precarious living but they are saved from despair by Eling's strong instinct of survival and by the support of the community, members of which look after each other in times of adversity.

At times nature comes to the rescue. When it pours with rain everything is made cleaner, the crusts and filth of the streets are washed away. Even Kampoon Street looks brighter. In the New Territories, visiting Adi's tomb, the family is surrounded by greenery and can breathe in the fresh air.

Above all Lin Tai-yi shows us, through her characters, that whatever the condition people live in, the human spirit cannot be crushed. Eling adapts to all the blows and arrows of fortune with fortitude; Riri is tough like her mother, but harder to read. Of the three she is the most emotionally introverted. But even though deserted by Sunny because of her pregnancy, she remains defiant blaming herself for the predicament she is in and determined to pull herself and the family out of it. Lam is the dreamer and artist, constantly pondering on reality:

*He looked up at the stars and wondered that they existed, without foreknowledge of the next day, next year, or millennium, and thought, why should he worry? Maybe a brick will fall from a building and knock me dead on the street one day. There is no pattern, no logical development of life, no need of mind, only the body going on its own way, demanding to be fed and washed and clad.*[lxviii]

His stoicism enables him to get on even in the dreary surrounds of the factory where he finds a temporary job.

Kampoon Street is not the most salubrious place in the world but it has turned out to be not a bad training ground for facing life's considerable challenges.

# Chapter 7
# The Monkey King and Sour Sweet:
# Timothy Mo

The physical world of Austin Coates and Timothy Mo is the same Hong Kong and rural New Territories of the 1950s but the perspective of each of them is different. While Coates is pondering on the nature of the Chinese and Chinese culture from the magistrate's bench, Timothy Mo is in the midst of the world he says is characterised by Cantonese bluntness. That is not to say that ambiguity and elusiveness do not colour the motives and behaviour of Mo's characters in *The Monkey King* but rather that he is looking across, rather than down, at them. That viewpoint does not prevent Mo from making fun and satirising the behaviour and predicament of his creations, something that colours his entire work. Nevertheless, both Coates's and Mo's perspectives are views of a Chinese society which is set in the superficial, colonial wrapping of post-war Hong Kong. They are both, in that way, utterly local.

Timothy Mo is himself a displaced Hong Kong boy. Born to an English mother and a Chinese father, he first went to an English school in Hong Kong before being sent at the age of ten to school in England where he was anglicized in the traditional way that those of 'Empire background' were – in public school and then at Oxford. His first venture into the world of words was as a journalist for the *New Statesman* and the *Boxing News,* the latter reflecting his early boxing training by a certain Mr Tingle when he was a young boy in Hong Kong. Before long his true vocation, as a novelist, came to the fore. His success was marked by a series of awards for different works but the critics never fully got to grips with a writer who seems enigmatic and at one remove, the outsider who has come into the fold but whose identity remains ambiguous.

*The Monkey King,* first published in 1978, was the first of a series of novels but the only one entirely set in his childhood home. Later Mo set his monumental historical novel, *An Insular Possession* (1986) in the period of the opium war and the acquisition of Hong Kong by the British in the 1840s. Although *The Monkey King* could only have been written by a local boy, Mo was subsequently becoming disenchanted with what he saw as a certain rigidity in Chinese culture and announced that he was not a Chinese writer, a stance that raises questions about his own identity. Unlike some post-colonial writers who questioned their use of the English language as their means of expression, Mo was an English writer without question although the *The Monkey King* and *Sour Sweet* are replete with Cantonese colloquial expressions and allusions.

So far as the image of *The Monkey King* is concerned, it is taken from classical Chinese mythology. A Ming dynasty novel, *Hsi Yu Chi* by the author Wu Cheng, tells the story of a monk in search of Buddhist wisdom in India who is accompanied by a monkey with supernatural powers. The monkey has been imprisoned for 500 years after rebelling against heaven. The creature is represented as a figure with magical powers, a trickster, a rebel, as well as a comic figure. The symbolism of the monkey is therefore powerfully grounded in Chinese tradition at the highly significant moment of the introduction of Buddhism from India.

The hero of *The Monkey King* is Wallace Nolasco, a Macau boy of Chinese ethnicity. The story begins in neighbouring Macau rather than in Hong Kong. Like Ignatius (Kwan Po), the half-caste servant in Austin Coates's *City of Broken Promises,* Wallace is burdened by his mixed background in a colonial society based on the notion of the racial superiority of Europeans. Ignatius speaks perfect English; Wallace speaks perfect Cantonese although he affects to despise the brash dialect of it that is spoken in Macau. The latter pretence is a significant way in which Wallace asserts his superiority over other locals although ironically it disqualifies him from respect among the local Chinese who still regard themselves as a cut above all foreigners. Despite the perceived differences of background, Wallace is committed, in an arranged marriage, to May Ling, the daughter of a successful and grasping Chinese entrepreneur who lives in a mansion in Robinson Road on Hong Kong Island.

Wallace leaves Macau to join his wife's family in Hong Kong. He enters the Poon household with some trepidation. Not only is his position financially precarious (he has been tricked out of the dowry agreed between the families) but he is ostracised both by members of the family and the servants, the latter especially regarding him as an intruder. Prominent among the servants are two *amahs*, Ah Doh and Ah Ling, who in the traditional way exert huge influence on the running of the household, particularly in their supervision of the family's meals, a pervasive Cantonese preoccupation. Meals are a scramble in a free-for-all as chopsticks become the weapons of attack. The *amahs* first serve a soup with great punctuality before bringing out other dishes. The next stage of the meal is less organised:

*By contrast with the ordered distribution of the soup, the eggs constituted an anarchic free-for-all, due respect paid to Mr Poon's precedence. Apart from this consideration, the only factors regulating the disappearance of the eggs were the reach of the participants and their facility with their chopsticks.*[lxix]

This is something Wallace is just not used to; he was too slow to join in the battle at the table. Moreover, in the jostle to reach for the vital white rice accompanying the main dishes, he finds that the *amahs* have served him only burnt portions, something that hunger makes him adapt to eating with relish.

The son of the household, Ah Lung, is an awkward character, always ready to assert his position in the hierarchy though he himself seems a reprobate with little interest in doing anything constructive. He annoys Wallace by playing on his intimacy with May Ling, showing scant regard for the fact that she is now married to Wallace. Then there are the half-sisters of May Ling who, in the Oriental manner, simply ignore a man whom they also regard as an intruder. Wallace has more success with Clarence and Hogan, the schoolboy members of the family whom he takes out to see horror movies. The most sympathetic and welcoming person in the household is Mrs Poon herself who has mellowed into a benign middle age.

Mr Poon himself is an unsavoury figure who rules autocratically over the bizarre and dysfunctional household in Robinson Road. Anxious that May Ling, daughter of the second concubine, should not be left on the shelf without a husband, he agrees to the marriage with Wallace as a solution but at first has little time for his Macanese son-in-law who is just another mouth to feed. A cunning and adaptive entrepreneur, he gradually begins to realise that Wallace may be of use to him in his various dubious business enterprises.

Although Mr Poon's unpleasant side is all too evident, there is a stolid reliability about him. Moreover, he is a careful observer of Chinese customs. This is made evident during the festival of C'hing Ming when there is a duty to visit ancestral graves, burn counterfeit money and clean the burial plots. It is a hot and dusty day; the cemetery is laid out on a hill where:

*the graves were cut into the hillside in steeply ascending terraces, platforms so narrow that unsubstantiated rumour had it that coffins had to be slotted into the cheaper lots in an upright position.*[lxx]

Mr Poon is careful to observe the necessary rituals even when it involves the considerable physical effort of climbing the steep hillside where the graves are located. However, while he concerns himself with the whole suckling pig that has been brought along for a picnic, the other family members attend to the tedious job of the weeding the heavily overgrown ground around the graves under the scorching sun. The neglect of the plots has been a result of Mr Poon's economising on tips for the groundsmen who look after the cemetery. He also tries to bargain with the hawkers at the entrance gates where they gather to ply visitors with drinks and snacks, but the tradesmen are canny and refuse to lower their prices. Only Wallace is lured into buying sour plums which make him extremely thirsty as no doubt the hawkers have foreseen. The family visit to the cemetery very much conjures up the local, Chinese atmosphere on a special festival day.

As the narrative develops Mr Poon seems to age. His opinion of Wallace also changes – the initial distrust of his son-in-law is mellowed by the notion that after all he may be a useful contributor to the family legacy if carefully guided. For his part, Wallace gains greater confidence in his dealings with the patriarch, sometimes challenging him on particular decisions he has made. The scheme they dream up together is that Wallace should enter the Public Works Department so as to influence the granting of contracts to Mr Poon's business. At this point Mo takes a swipe at the easy-going corruption of the Hong Kong colonial service.

The departmental head of Public Works is Allardyce, a *bon vivant* in the expatriate style of the period. Allardyce's life is a round of social events with the enigmatic Mabel, possibly a high-class prostitute, lurking in the background. Parties, excursions and banquets dominate the days; there is little time for attention to the details of administration. Mabel, born in Shanghai, claims an exotic connection with a white Russian princess; she is an extravagant dresser clad in the most expensive fashions available. Her flair for dressing is matched by an array of jewellery. She has:

*jade rings of the darkest and most even hue – more precious than diamonds – on every finger and each of her long thumbs, pendulous ear-rings, gold brooches hammered and spun into butterflies, turtles and mermaids, ropes of pearls, layers of bracelets. She clanked as she walked in a cloud of French perfume.*[lxxi]

Although Mabel is devoted to a distant cousin of Wallace, Pippy, she keeps a distance from Wallace, reflecting her own insecurity in the hierarchy of colonial society where the *gweilos,* or foreigners, dominate. Pippy herself is more confident, having been to the British King George V School in Ho Man Tin. Wallace meets Pippy and Mabel in the cavernous, shadowy ballroom of the Repulse Bay Hotel hoping to make allies of Mabel and her husband, Mr Poon's sleeping partner. But he does not succeed. Things begin badly when Mabel puts Wallace down for his choice of having milk instead of lemon in his tea; whatever hopes he had of gaining support against Mr Poon evaporate as the afternoon wears on.

Wallace is soon installed in the Public Works Department as a reliable local boy with a useful, direct link to Mr Poon's company. Both sides are set to benefit from this liaison. At first business runs smoothly proving profitable both for Allardyce and Mr Poon. However, there is a sudden jolt to their dubious relationship. Repair works carried out by the company on a construction site collapse in the rain. An official inquiry is launched. Both sides agree that Wallace is better off away from the office during the investigation so he and May Ling are packed off to the rural New Territories of Austin Coates. Although the circumstances of their banishment are not propitious, they eventually offer a new lease of life for Wallace, removed from the claustrophobic atmosphere of the house in Robinson Road.

At first, he and May Ling are isolated, living on the edge of the local community rather than being part of it. Rural life takes some getting used to. Sleeping on hard beds with straw mats, they are disturbed by a constant chorus of cicadas and croaking frogs. An unpleasant odour from the nearby factory fills the air. Their house is on the edge of the village; not being involved in any agricultural work separates them from daily contact with most of the villagers.

The organisation of the village is a highly traditional set up with heads of households meeting in the ancestral hall to sort out local business. At the head of the village hierarchy is the headman, who politely ignores the newcomers, the reason for whose presence in the village is not clear to the locals. His dominant position in the village, confirmed during the Japanese occupation, is virtually impregnable. Another important character is the owner of the tea shop whose premises serve as the community's social centre. He has risen from a humble background of the so called 'slave class', or people who had been in bondage. His position is secure as head of the night watch, in effect the village police force. The headman cannot afford to ignore him.

Bordering on the village are tracts of land belonging to the fierce Hakkas, an arrangement that inevitably leads to territorial disputes of the sort so familiar to Austin Coates when he was the Special Magistrate. After various skirmishes between the two communities, a contest between them is arranged in which each side fields a formidable team of young men to battle it out in a ball game.

Meanwhile Wallace and May Ling have the chance to enjoy the open space of the countryside, a welcome freedom from the urban confines of the life on Hong Kong Island. Rambling beyond the village walls, they discover green hills which abound in wildlife: barking deer and wild pigs roam freely. Lichen covered rocks, small streams and bamboo groves add an enchanted feeling to their wanderings.

However, one of their excursions does not go well, especially for Chinese people, highly superstitious about the treatment of their ancestors. By chance they enter a cave which is used by the villagers as an ancestral tomb. Wallace enters without realising this and treads on human bones, all that remains of those buried there. Both he and May Ling are utterly shocked and terrified of the bad luck that will befall them because of the desecration, unintentional though it has been. As appeasement for his behaviour Wallace agrees to May Ling's suggestion to leave his watch as a token seeking forgiveness.

Away at last from the complex machinations of the family, the pair begin to grow closer together, living more like a married couple. Quite suddenly their semi-detached existence from the community comes to an end. A violent typhoon sweeps over the whole area, torrential rain causing the paddy fields to become a lake and even diminishing the elevation of the village. The water level fed from the ocean is salty and ruined the first crop of rice from which the villagers derive their living. At the same time the desecration of the ancestral tomb is discovered but to Wallace's relief, the villagers ascribe to interference by malevolent forces which would need to be placated by exorcism. When the priest and monks arrived, they declared the *feng shui* of the village to be disastrous but offered no practical solutions to the villagers' pressing problems. In fact, no one had any idea of how to deal with the crisis.

May Ling reminds Wallace of his engineering background. As a plan begins to form in his mind, he makes an expedition in a boat to measure the depth at which blocked sluice gates are sunk. At home he draws up a map showing all the places where the sluices are buried. He comes to the conclusion that small explosive charges would open the gates up, drawing the flood water away from the fields. Although the headman cannot understand the mechanics of the scheme, in the absence of any other, he agrees to it. The scheme works, leading to the successful draining of the main field so that a second crop of rice can be planted. The villagers' main source of income is restored. Meanwhile Wallace proposes leaving the other flooded field as a lake which he imaginatively suggests can become a tourist attraction for urbanites seeking a tranquil setting for bathing and fishing. Both the draining scheme and his idea for tourism work. Wallace assumes an entirely new status in the village; from an unwelcome outsider, he becomes a hero lauded by one and all.

On this high note, the couple return to civilisation such as it is, in the Poon household. Mr Poon himself passes way and Wallace is now obviously suited and capable of taking over the headship of the family. The book ends with a bizarre dream sequence: Wallace is at a formal Chinese banquet, ivory chopsticks and curved spoons are laid out on the table in the centre of which is a box, covered by a cloth. When the draping is removed, a cage is exposed in which a young monkey 'wrinkled bloodless lips back, baring its teeth in rage and terror'.[lxxii] It seems to know its fate for in a short while it is beaten to death and pulped into an edible mass which the guests begin to devour. Wallace suddenly wakes up to hear the rain pattering on the bedroom window.

Whether this dénouement is meant to symbolise Wallace's triumph over the trickster monkey of the legend or not what is certain is that Wallace has come of age. But what explains his gradual ascent to maturity? Is it by conformity to the values of the extended Chinese family or has he held his ground as a rebel against its norms? The answer seems to lie between the two.

Wallace had arrived at the Poon household as an outsider. He is treated rather haughtily by Mr Poon himself and ostracized by most of the family, only really succeeding in forming an avuncular relationship with the two schoolboys. The *amahs*, always quietly powerful in the traditional Chinese household, made great play of Wallace's inferior status. His relationship with May Ling was tenuous even though they are married and only developed into a partnership during their time in exile in the rural community. But gradually things changed. Mr Poon began to see advantages in using Wallace's talents for the business. Their relationship, lacking any sentimental base, developed out of mutual self-interest. Wallace's self-confidence increased after the success of his intervention in village affairs. On return to the city, he is ready to assume the role of patriarch after Mr Poon's death though we expect him to perform the role in a more modern, and less tyrannical, way.

Two distinct features of *The Monkey King* set it out as a novel that has a uniquely Hong Kong feel about it. The first is in Mo's use of dialogue. Throughout the narrative, the characters speak a kind of Pidgin English, utterly familiar to local ears. Certain expressions from Cantonese, such as the ubiquitous *wah* (pronounced with a long, extended 'a') indicating wonder or surprise, with a tinge of admiration, counterbalanced by *Eiyah*, 'heavens, oh dear' are suitably authentic colloquial expressions. But Mo does not spare the Chinese community from his satirical knife. At Chinese New Year red packets of 'lucky' money are given to single people after they demand it in a blunt verse addressed to the donors, hoping that the sum they give will be substantially more than a dollar. There is nothing too refined about this ceremony.

Another, more visual feature of the novel is the reference to all the landmarks of the colony – the Star Ferry, the Peak Tram, Nathan Road. While all the characters in the narrative may use the Star Ferry – whether upstairs in the comfortable first-class cabins or downstairs in steerage – few of them will have access to the prestige establishments like the Hong Kong Club or the Peninsula Hotel which only the colonial expatriates like Allardyce or leading businessmen, frequent. These landmarks are seen through the eyes of the silent majority but they remind us that this Chinese city has a superficial colonial superstructure. We tour every part of the island and Kowloon, up and down Garden Road, to Wanchai with its seedy dancing halls, to the kitsch of Tiger Balm Gardens, Aberdeen's floating restaurants and even Stanley prison. As we are taken through the backstreets, we hear the sound of mahjong cubes crashing and the scent of joss sticks perfume the air. It is a curious and exotic mix that captures the authentic flavour Hong Kong of the 1950s.

It also reminds us of Mo's assertion that he is not a Chinese writer. Whatever that denial entails there is no doubt that *The Monkey King* could only have been written by someone steeped in the Cantonese culture of Hong Kong. Another of Mo's novels may clarify the enigma about his 'Chinese-ness'. Although *Sour Sweet* is set in London's Chinatown it is as authentically Cantonese as *The Monkey King*. One of the characters in the book symbolically wears two watches, one showing English time, the other Hong Kong time. The novel opens on an ambiguous note raising the typically Mo dilemma of identity:

*The Chens had been living in the UK for four years, which was long enough to have lost their place in the society from which they had emigrated but not long enough to feel comfortable in the new.*[lxxiii]

In fact, the Chens never do feel comfortable in the 'fan gweilo' world they live in but rather have adapted to it, gradually improving their lives by dint of hard work. Chen is a restaurant worker who spends the greatest part of his day slaving away in the kitchen or serving mainly Western customers at table. It is a business run in the Chinese fashion, with everyone taking part as if members of an extended family. Many of the waiters have come from the same village. After a hectic day, all the employees sit round a table to a late dinner of soup, rice and pork. When Chen leaves towards midnight for the council flat in which the family live, he takes a short cut to the tube through an alleyway which is strewn with rubbish and rotting vegetables that could be a backstreet in Wanchai or Mongkok. Although he is full from the meal at work Lily, his wife, forces him to sit down to a bowl of rich, home-made soup. 'Husband' (Mo leaves out the indefinite article in all his references to Chen), dutifully eats it. The Chen household consists of Lily, her sister ('Moon Lily') and a two-year-old son, Man Kee whom the aunt has been suborned to help look after.

Lily is a strong-minded Kwantung lady of 'superabundant energies'[lxxiv] whom Chen met and married in their New Territories village. Unusually for a woman she was trained in her childhood in the martial arts, learning to fight like a Shantung boxer, kicking her opponent before a punch. Her father, a martial arts instructor, disappointed at not having a son, brought her up as if she was one. It was tough, lonely upbringing which clearly left its mark on her character. Lily is an ambitious achiever but as the narrative develops, we discover a *ying* or feminine side to her character as she struggles to keep the family afloat by thrifty household management. She exhibits the traditional, humble qualities of a worthy wife devoted not only to her immediate family but also to the duty of sending remittances to Chen's ageing parents in Hong Kong.

Chen himself is a stolid, reliable sort, if somewhat inscrutable. He accepts his fate as a minor player in the Chinese underworld society to which the restaurant is inextricably connected through the criminal network operating in Soho. But that does not make him happy. Nor does he enjoy the company of city slickers like Roman Fok who sneers at the New Territory waiters, reminding us of the alienation of rural/urban life noticed by Austin Coates from the magistrate's bench. When Roman Fok tries to annoy Chen, Chen simply ignores the provocation showing no sign of his inner disdain, regarding Fok's stories of sexual adventures as disgusting. Chen's face remains expressionless. Instead of joining in the chatter, he goes off with his friend, Mr Lo, for an afternoon break to watch horror movies.

Chen's talents are in cooking and gardening. He grows much of the produce that the family use for themselves and the business once he has quit his work at the restaurant and set himself up as a take-away in a dilapidated garage in the suburbs. This heralds a happier period for the whole family, as by dint of hard work and toil, the business begins to succeed. Lily is at the centre of the enterprise, driving it forward relentlessly. Her great dream is that her son will succeed and take care of her and husband once they are old and infirm. Her sometimes abrasive manner makes for a volatile relationship with her sister who, in her own quiet way, is quite stubborn. Moon Lily ('Mui') seems to have a different outlook on living in England; she is careful to recognise individual customers and her more open manner goes down well with the burly English men who come to collect their take-away. Nevertheless, she makes a contribution to the family well-being as is expected of her, adding considerably to the profits of the business until one day she has to be laid off due to an unexpected and unexplained pregnancy.

Lily herself is more introverted in the Chinese way and we see the English through her eyes. She instinctively believes in Chinese superiority and finds that all:

*Occidental faces looked the same compared to the infinite variety of Cantonese physiognomies: rascally, venerable, pretty, raffish, bumpkin, scholarly.*[lxxv]

While anxious to make the best of life in her new surroundings, Lily's efforts are directed entirely at keeping the small Chen family together, untainted from foreign influence. Once her son reaches school age, she makes sure that he is also enlisted for Chinese classes once a week in a backstreet of Chinatown where children are sent to learn traditional Chinese calligraphy and literature. Lily is re-assured by the discipline that she finds in the makeshift school which contrasts with the laxity of behaviour in English schools. This discipline and training of character seems to have little to do with acquiring knowledge or encouraging creativity. It does, however, instil veneration for the elderly, something which Lily, like traditional Chinese parents, hopes to instil in Man Kee. Her attitude enables Mo to satirise Chinese classical education which demands respect for teachers and for learning by rote.

The Chens' social life is limited to their association with a Mrs Law, a rich Chinese widow who lives on her own with her servant, Ah Jik. Mrs Law is described as 'old school' who is politely reticent yet accommodating. Despite perceiving a difference in social standing, Mrs Law becomes an adopted mother to the family, taking in Moon Lily during her pregnancy and eventually marrying Mr Lo, Mr Chen's pal from the restaurant. This extended family growth is nothing unusual in Chinese culture where aunts and uncles may take on the role of parents with children brought up together regardless of who their parents actually were. Gifts of food from the Chen sisters and luxuries in return from Mrs Law build up the relationship in which whatever reservations may be held on both sides, nothing is actually said to disturb the community they have formed together. And Ah Jik, the *amah,* silently observes it all without any comment.

In the meantime, a much darker sub plot to the novel is developed in Mo's depiction of the activities of the triad societies – criminal gangs of a Mafia-type tendency – who fight it out for control of the lucrative drug trade in Chinatown. In one of their dens lurk:

*tough looking boys…with an inclination towards pale corduroy or darker leather jackets, their long hair brushing the collar in soft black spikes. They had a fashion for wearing heavy signet rings, two on each of the fingers that were missing on Ma's right hand, in what might have been construed as a tribute to the older man.*[lxxvi]

These are bad boys (*lan jai*) who at the behest of Triad leaders like Red Cudgel and White Paper Fan would attack and maim anyone they were ordered to. The Triad societies thrive on the drug trade, particularly heroin claiming descent from the Hung fighters who emerged in the time of the Emperor Kang Hsi during the Ming dynasty. The sworn enemies of Red Cudgel's group were another gang, the 14-K; each gang fights to control the lucrative trade in heroin. Mixed together among the tough bullies were some surprisingly sophisticated people, like Ricky Lam. Ricky began his career as a shoeshine boy in Hong Kong and through various stages, including that of debt collector, ascended to being a smooth-talking trade union leader. When he left Hong Kong for Britain, he has not forgotten by the shoeshine children 'who had loved him and fought for the right to clean his already shining boots, and not only for the huge tips he gave'.[lxxvii] At the other end of the spectrum is the refined and well-educated Miranda who had been to school in Cheltenham but nevertheless discreetly serves tea at the Triad meetings.

The leaders themselves are depicted as cunning and ruthless who will stop at nothing, including the extermination of their rivals, if that was necessary. The portrayal of this violent, clannish world where newcomers are taught the fiercest martial arts, introduces a dark side to Mo's portrayal of the Cantonese character. Far from being a passive, inscrutable people, these representatives of the race are as aggressive and inhuman as any counterparts in the Western society in which they find themselves. Their connections with Hong Kong remain strong; it is not a part of society that Austin Coates would have found congenial.

As in the narrative of *The Monkey King,* Mo's interlacing of colloquial Cantonese expressions adds a local, Hong Kong flavour to the telling of *Sour Sweet*. The ubiquitous expressions of surprise or inquiry *hah* and *wah* are balanced up with words of thanks, *doh jeh* and praise *gum ho wan* such good fun, so well played. Food of course has to figure prominently – *chow fan* and *chow mein* are served and toasts (*yum sing*) made to the hosts. Much of the constant comparison of Chinese and English culture is highlighted in the use of this everyday language.

Chen's experiences in the restaurant and later in his own business; Lily's determined management and sister Mui's attempts at adapting, all echo the theme of identity. Whatever the particular situation of the three family members, they are struggling to come to terms with an alien culture. Applying Chinese custom and practice reserves them a space for a while but it cannot protect them from a gradual loss of pure Chinese identity. While the story develops with the two strands – the family tale and the Triad one – apparently separated, the denouement turns out to be a tragic intertwining of the two. Chen vanishes in an act of settling scores by the brotherhood. Lily rationalises this in the only way she can by imagining that he has moved on to greener pastures, perhaps abroad, but not forgotten his family. Once a month a remittance arrives – sent anonymously by the Triad society – which Lily takes to have been sent by Chen from wherever he has fled. Not knowing the source of the income, she is able to cling on to her belief that it comes from Chen. Moreover, the promise is that Man Kee will take over family leadership once he grows up. She may have lost her husband but she still has her son whom no one can take away from her.

# Chapter 8
# The Piano Teacher: Janice Y K Lee

Janice Y K Lee is a Korean writer who was brought up in Hong Kong in the 1970s. In an interview she explained:

*I am Korean, so I was never a local in the strict sense of the word, but Hong Kong is so international that it never really mattered. People wash up in Hong Kong and stay, and create new lives for themselves. It's that type of place.*[lxxviii]

During her childhood a British influence predominated, particularly as she started attending an English school, later switching to an American one. This was a prelude to her continuing education in the United States where she eventually read English and American literature at Harvard. Thereafter she moved to become a journalist in New York, editing well-known magazines for a number of years. She recorded the importance of understanding what is involved in bringing a book to production, the prerogative of editors and being in a community of people who valued words and were devoted to books. After further studies at Hunter College, she began to write her first novel, *the Piano Teacher* (2009).

Throughout her time in America, the image of Hong Kong remained vividly in her imagination. She says she had been tantalised:

*by glimpses of the old colonial order [in Hong Kong] and how it existed in an uneasy proximity with local society, both high and low.*[lxxix]

The mixed identity of the British and Chinese Hong Kong of the 1970s had not changed greatly since the days of Han Suyin and Martin Booth in the 1950s; it was still the same society through which Austin Coates had moved seamlessly.

The colonial surface, with its glitter and somewhat provincial social life hid a city of Chinese energy and colour, sounds and smells. Only a few, bold individuals moved between these different worlds.

Janice Lee moved back to Hong Kong in 2005 (though she was there in 1997 to witness the handover of the colony to China). On the surface some things had changed: the term 'Royal' had been dropped from the title of many institutions; the currency looked different. But other things, like the name of streets, remained reassuringly familiar: Gloucester, Pottinger, and Connaught. Those names represented the colonial history of the city, now entering a new phase of development. Even so she feels that no part of China looks or feels like Hong Kong.

The plot of *the Piano Teacher* is complex: two different stories are told in the novel, one in Hong Kong at the time of the Japanese invasion; the other in the hectic period of the 1950s after the war. The link between the two plots is in the enigmatic character of Will Truesdale, a young Englishman who is the hero of the first part and, in a certain sense, the anti-hero of the second. The main narrative, set in the 1950s, centres on the character of Claire Pendelton, a young English woman who is married to Martin, an engineer in the Department of Water Services. Martin's job is to supervise the building of a new reservoir at Tai Lam Cheung. Claire has been warned by her mother that the Chinese are 'unscrupulous, conniving people'[lxxx] as she sails away from Southampton on the *P & O Canton*. But she is happy to escape a humdrum life in drearily rationed post-war England. When the ship finally arrives at the dockside in Kowloon the passengers are entertained to a noisy reception; a band plays and streamers are flung from the decks to the crowded pier below where vendors, shouting their wares, mingled with uniformed officials waiting for the new arrivals. A clink of champagne glasses fills the air: it is a lively introduction to the exotic world that Claire is about to enter.

Claire is depicted as a shy character somewhat overwhelmed by the colonial setting, a far cry from suburban England. She needs a job and, as a trained pianist, is soon employed by the Chens, a rich Chinese family who live in great luxury in May Road, to teach their daughter, Locket, piano. The Chens are connected to everyone of importance and their moneyed status gives them entry to the expatriate world. They frequent all the colonial haunts – the Peninsula Hotel, the upstairs reserve at the Gloucester, Lane Crawford the exclusive department store, the Jockey Club. They order cream cakes from *Tkachenko* and throw lavish parties for expatriates and rich businessmen. Everyone jostles to be invited.

Melody Chen is a typical mother of an upper-class Hong Kong family known as *tai tais*. She spends her time lunching at fashionable places, gossiping with her friends and being chauffeured around in limousines. She is always dressed in the latest fashion. Her family background, like so many of her type, is in Shanghai, although she herself was educated in England and America. Victor Chen is a somewhat elusive character. Dressed in smart pin-striped suits with neat silk handkerchiefs in his breast pocket, he exudes an air of know-how and success. When Claire expresses her wish to learn Cantonese, he warns her that the nine tones of the language often defeat Europeans, especially those who are used to English which is so much simpler to pronounce. When Claire tells her husband Martin that Chen does not seem the typical 'Chinaman', he warns her not to use that expression which justifies the Chinese belief that foreigners are clumsy and rude. He tells her that Chen is in the top drawer of Hong Kong society; she needs to be careful in dealing with the family.

Locket's progress at learning to play the piano is annoyingly slow. Claire soon realises that the girl is not interested in music and never practices in between lessons. She remains polite but bored, giggling in an irritating manner to disguise her embarrassment when she is scolded by her teacher. Neither of her parents seems much troubled by her lack of commitment; having their daughter learn piano is just for show. Meanwhile Claire, on her regular visits to the mansion, succumbs to kleptomania, gradually stealing different items from the Chen household from small porcelain objects to expensive, silk scarves which Melody has carelessly thrown around. It seems that her behaviour is unnoticed by the brigade of house boys and *amahs* employed in the Chens' mansion.

As in all Hong Kong households the *amahs* play a significant part: Trudy Chen is entirely spoilt by her Ah Lok and Ah Sing, her two *amahs* who are at hand to pamper to her every need. She is correspondingly protective of them even if they fall short of doing the domestic chores as well as they should. As Claire is a mere employee the two *amahs* consider her as an outsider who can be largely ignored. In her own home, Claire herself is uneasy with Yu Ling, her own servant. She can't break through the barrier that divides them and is unable to induce the kind of loyalty that others seem to manage with ease. Her reserve also makes it difficult for her to settle down in the fevered atmosphere of Hong Kong society where people scramble to make money, under the constant threat of invasion from China. She lacks the confidence to mix in the sometimes-aggressive social milieu, feeling snubs real or imagined. Within her is a turmoil of emotion:

*She wanted to be someone else. The old Claire seemed provincial, ignorant. She had been to a party at Government House, sipped champagne at the Gripps while women she knew twirled around in silky dresses. She had her nose pressed up against the glass and was watching a different world. She could not name it but she felt as if she was about to be revealed, as if there was another Claire inside, waiting to come out. In these few hours in the morning, dressed in someone else's finery, she could pretend she was part of it...*[lxxxi]

It is only when she meets Will Treusdale that her life starts to assume a livelier pattern, though a rather hidden one. Will is an enigmatic character: although hired by the Chens as a chauffeur, he is rarely to be seen at the Chen home. Having moved to be closer to the May Road mansion of his employers, he misses the livelier, local atmosphere of Happy Valley where he had been living before. Will has been in Hong Kong for some time, including the years of the Japanese occupation when he was interned in Stanley Camp. He claims to be delighted to meet someone, like Claire, who has not yet been jaded by Hong Kong life, with its pretentious social rounds. When Claire tells him that she has wandered about the streets of Kowloon on her own, he says he likes the idea of an English woman who ventures outside the areas of Central and the Peak.

Janice Lee intersperses her tale of the 1950s with flashbacks to a decade earlier centring her tale around the flamboyant character of Trudy, a Eurasian *grande dame* and cousin of Melody Chen. In the first scene, set in September 1941, Trudy is anxious to attend an end of summer party being given by Manley Haverford in a spacious house near the sea even though she regards him as an impossible bigot. She is accompanied by Will Treusdale to the party and, under her spell, he plunges into the sea with her. Their affair has begun in earnest.

Trudy once again exemplifies the dilemma of the Eurasian caught up in a colonial hierarchy as we have seen was the case for Han Suyin and for Austin Coates's fictional characters. A Eurasian is not Chinese enough for the Chinese and not European enough for Europeans. Trudy, born of a Portuguese mother and a Chinese father, is a robust character who is not put out by the underlying tone of rejection veiled in a hypocritical pretence of acceptance. She is delighted by a newspaper editorial which she reads out to Will:

*The Eurasian is a problem in all British colonies. The term is applied loosely to the offspring of all mixed marriages and their children etc. etc. That Britain and some other occidental Powers chose to victimize the Eurasian rather than accept him and make him use his qualities is astonishing to students of the question. The Eurasian could be a great help to these Powers, contributing valuable liaison between the ruling nation and the native population.*[lxxxii]

In a later episode of the main story, Claire also encounters the same prejudice from a long-standing member of the English community who says there is something sad and incomplete about Eurasians. Claire responds with a polite put off:

*I find them [Eurasians] very attractive, actually, with their beautiful skin and golden eyes and hair. When I was first in Hong Kong, I did find them odd-looking but now I think they are splendid.*[lxxxiii]

She is told that she is a romantic, which is not meant as a compliment.

Trudy herself is a *bon viveur* frequenting spots like the Parisian Grill, oblivious of the warning signs all around. The talk in that autumn of 1941 is all about the preparations for war, and among a small elite of the administration, what is to be done with the Crown Collection, a hoard of valuable *objets d'art*, jewellery and artefacts acquired by the colonial government. When the evacuation of women and children begins, Trudy shrugs off the idea of going to Australia on her British passport. Instead, she designs outfits for the Volunteer Corps flippantly suggesting that Will, the perfect male specimen, should be the model.

Gradually the atmosphere darkens as the Japanese invasion begins with a bombing at Kai Tak airport of the remaining British aircraft. Air raids begin to affect different parts of colony; Kowloon is besieged by the advancing Japanese army. In one incident, Will is hit by flying debris; the companion he is with is killed. Trudy and Will escape to Angeline's house on the Peak which remains safe if under siege. Although Angeline and Trudy have stacks of ready cash which they use in dangerous forays to buy food, they start to run out of provisions until the anglicised Dominick, Trudy's cousin, turns up with a fresh supply. No one asks where he has got the goods from. Soon the servants of the house disappear, though they are honest enough not to have stolen provisions which were lying in the kitchen.

The tense, uncertain atmosphere of the last days of the battle of Hong Kong is well captured in the novel. Trudy's apparent insouciance is a cover up; her way of dealing with an impossible and unpredictable situation. The streets of the city, normally bustling, are empty. People rush out to buy what they can before hurrying home. Looters make the most of abandoned shops and stalls. Meanwhile Japanese planes drone overhead dropping propaganda leaflets which urge the local population to support their Oriental brothers. Angeline points out that the atrocities in China have been brushed aside by this spurious propaganda. On Christmas Day, the three sing carols and devour the food Dominick has brought them, not yet knowing that the Hong Kong forces have surrendered. Parties, with people still dressed in evening wear are planned for New Year's Eve. A few weeks later all British, American and European allies are rounded up in Murray Parade Ground, military personnel separated from civilians who are consigned to Stanley Prison Camp.

Trudy is a person to whom the rules have never applied. She remains outside prison, striking up a relationship with Otsubo, the Japanese commander which enables her to get Will a temporary release from Stanley Camp for a short while. He is even entertained by Otsubo as it is believed he knows the whereabouts of the Crown Collection. Cousin Dominick is also a collaborator and even lover of the commander. As her influence declines Trudy's fate is sealed: she disappears without trace before the end of the Japanese occupation. Meanwhile Dominick has fled to neutral Macau.

Returning to the main story of the 1970s, Claire's fate is an unhappy one. She is no longer with her husband, Martin or Will, her lover. Instead, she is driven into a hermetical life of her own, living in squalid conditions in an unfashionable part of town. Rejected by her own people, she is regarded as an eccentric 'gwai por' (devil lady) by the locals among whom she now lives.

In Janice Lee's second novel, *The Expatriates* (2016), we move to a later period, marked by cell phones and emails which characterises the global world inhabited by the expatriate community in the 1990s. This time we are invited to observe the American section of the broader community whose life style of parties and launch picnics differ little from the rest of the expatriate world and bears a remarkable resemblance to the style of life of earlier periods. Although several of the characters in the novel have a Korean background or connection, reflecting Janice Lee's own origins, they tend to be trapped in a small, inward-looking society in which there is little mixing across ethnic divides.

The tragic core of the novel, involving the disappearance of a young child of an American family, takes place in Seoul where the family are on holiday. Young 'G' the boy who has been abducted is said to have had a more Asian appearance than his siblings and was supposed to be being looked after by Mercy, his American/Korean carer. There are harrowing scenes as the parents desperately search the city for him in vain. G has vanished for good.

Despite the incident taking place abroad, the novel is firmly based in Hong Kong. We are reminded that this is still an entirely colonial setting: ladies of leisure, pampered by servants (now Filipina rather than Cantonese), spend their time in hotel lounges, restaurants and at beach parties gossiping while their husbands are at work. This world is as stifling and claustrophobic as Claire found it:

*Hong Kong is so small that if you go out enough, you will run into every expat at some point in the same five restaurants people frequent. The restaurants change but the scene never does.*[lxxxiv]

Although the colony has a rainbow of nationalities that are thrown together, the mix between them is mainly confined to their children knowing one another in the international schools. Coming from every corner of the world, the attempt of the newly-arrived to break out of their own narrow circles seldom lasts for long.

*When she first moved to Hong Kong, [Margaret] thought she might make friends with the different nationalities she saw all around her. Her children's friends were Danish, Japanese, local Hong Kong. But after a few strained meals, she saw it was easier to stay with your kind. So, although she loathed the concept, she embraced the reality and became friends with the same people she would have known in America.*[lxxxv]

Some expatriates try to escape from the confines of this existence by moving to live in remote parts of the colony. Lantau, away from the glitz of Hong Kong, is one place where they can set themselves up in an alternative lifestyle on an island which has not been over-developed. Keeping bees and making jam, inconceivable on the Peak, are readily available in this setting.

Nevertheless, there had been some changes in the fabric of social life from the 1950s and 1960s. In a restaurant scene the appearance of a family is described:

*They look Indonesian or Malaysian, and the children range from five to ten or so. They have three maids trailing them, in matching uniforms. The mother, in head-to-toe designer wear of the most glittering kind, and the father, in shiny Adidas tracksuit, sit down and bring out their phones and start tapping on them. The five year plays on an iPad that one of the maids holds up for him, like a human tripod. Another maid massages hand cream onto the hands of the middle girl. The maids stand up, as if they are not allowed to sit. Everyone in the restaurant is staring at them.[lxxxvi]*

It is noticeable that the family, though in a chic place, is neither European nor American, but Asian. Ironically though, the entry of these newcomers into the previously segregated world of Austin Coates of Martin Booth, does not lead to their assimilation with other groups. They keep to themselves and are seen by others as different and unapproachable. A new divisiveness keeps people apart, although it is not enforced by the colonial administration. In one or two cases, the invisible barrier between the expatriates and the Chinese is crossed. The third main character in the novel, Hilary, like Joyce Booth before her, is without prejudice. She relies emotionally on her friendship with Olivia, a Chinese *grand dame* who, however, has also had an Ivy League education. Hilary is impressed by Chinese manners, especially at the table where everyone is polite:

*They serve others the choice bits first, would never dream of eating before a guest, never drink the last of the wine, fight to pay the bill. An admirable trait of Asian culture, but then you are horrified when you go back to the United States and it's a free-for-all and every man for himself.[lxxxvii]*

When Hilary feels alienated from the expatriate community, she is supported by Olivia's apparent disdain for its trappings. Olivia's character echoes something of the character of Trudy in the *Piano Teacher*: she is upper crust and confident enough with her own Chinese identity not to be concerned about being cut off from colonial society. For Hilary herself, exclusion rankles, Margaret's loss of her son and Mercy's guilt about how it happened, eventually bring the three women in the narrative together. They have to face life's ups and downs and move on, however complicated that may be in the tangled and divisive mix of Hong Kong society. They can only do that by relying on each other: their shared need leads eventually to a special bond being formed between them.

In a conversation about her Hong Kong stories, Janice Lee talks about an uneasy proximity of expatriate and Chinese society in Hong Kong which continued despite the approaching end of the colonial period. Her exploration of the elusive duality of Hong Kong's social fabric echoes the preoccupation of many previous writers. Despite the opportunities that the extensive mix of nationalities in Hong Kong provides, contact between people of different ethnicities tends to be limited to formal settings, such as the office. Even families like the Chens, outwardly Westernised, have few close European friends. Intrepid individuals who cross the divide between the different cultures do so at the cost of rejection by their own people. Those caught in between, the Eurasians, remain in a social limbo as they were in the 1950s.

# Chapter 9
# The White Ghost Girls: Alice Greenway

Although Alice Greenway spent only five years in Hong Kong as a girl, it was clearly a formative experience. When she returned to her native United States, she remarked that she still carried Hong Kong inside her. Of the various exotic places where she spent her childhood, it remained special to her. Her father, David Greenway, was a journalist, acting as war correspondent for *Time* magazine and the *Washington Post.* He is resurrected in Alice's novella, *White Ghost Girls*, as the photographer who was obsessed with recording the course of the war in Vietnam which reached a crescendo in 1967. Alice sets the story of her girlhood experience, with her sister Frankie, in the same year, in Hong Kong where their father would turn up from time to time on leave from Vietnam. Later Alice herself became a journalist, working for the *South China Morning Post.* She gained recognition as a writer and was listed for various prizes.

While war was raging in Vietnam, the Cultural Revolution in China was reaching a new level of ferocity. Once again Hong Kong seemed under threat from its mighty neighbour; refugees streamed in from the mainland as they had done several decades earlier in Austin Coates's time. While most sought a better way of life, others were infiltrators whose objective was to cause as much turbulence as possible in the colony. The girls learnt about the earlier heroism of Mao Tze Tung when he escaped from Jiangxi province with his fellow communists and embarked on the Long March, trekking 6,000 miles to Sichuan and Tibet. Alice is impressed that in those heroic days Mao had not worn his later uniform of starched shirt and pinching collar; he looked more like a hero with his wild and shaggy hair. But that was a far cry from the Cultural Revolution when bands of Red Guards ran amok, smashing everything in their way. Those who were sent to Hong Kong planted bombs in public places making life dangerous and insecure.

Nevertheless, the Hong Kong world in which the 'White Ghost Girls' were growing up is still the recognisable world of Suzie Wong or Martin Booth a decade or more earlier. The back alleys with rubbish thrown around; the steep streets, with laundry strung along bamboo poles leading into the old Chinese quarters; smoked-filled temples where white-hooded mourners burn offerings and wail for the dead. The streets are noisy thoroughfares with overhanging balconies stacked with shop signs and rattan bird cages. Alice is nostalgic from the very first page of the novel:

*Can you give me hot rain, mould-streaked walls, a sharpness that creeps into my clothes, infests my books? The smells of dried oysters, clove hair oil, tiger balm, joss sticks burning to Kuan Yin in the backroom of a Chinese amah? The feverish shriek of cicadas, the cry of black-eared kites? The translucent green of sun shining through elephant ear leaves?[lxxxviii]*

The family home is in fact far away from the urban bustle of the city's backstreets; the girls are brought up in the fresh air of Pokfulam with distant views of Lamma Island and Cheung Chau. At nearby Stanley they could watch the dragon boat races. The house is surrounded by trees; the family are in the middle floor while Mr Mok, the landlord lives below on the ground floor and some 'tai tais' or elderly widows of his late father, on the top floor. Thinking that Hong Kong was a safe place, 'an old-fashioned British enclave',[lxxxix] their father, like everyone else, had not anticipated that daily bomb explosions would become a commonplace.

By the summer scores of bombs had exploded – in trash cans, on park benches and even in cinemas. Not content with just planting them the Red Guards also attacked the police and British army patrols. Battles took place on the streets causing widespread disruption to daily life. Other sinister reminders of the turmoil going on in China itself were the bodies floating onto the shores of Hong Kong from the outer islands and river estuary of Canton. No one knew where the corpses had come from or what had happened to the victims. Each day brought a rash of rumours and generated renewed panic. Wealthy individuals planned their move abroad; businesses started to relocate.

At home the girls were sheltered from this turbulence. As in so many Hong Kong homes, the presiding presence was that of an *amah*, in this case called Ah Bing. She lived in a tiny room beyond the kitchen. Sitting on a small wooden stool, Ah Bing combs her long, thin black her over one shoulder, twisting a strand into a bun.

*She has a wide, kind face: strong cheekbones, a flat nose, and generous, long-lobed ears. Good-luck Buddha ears, she calls them. Luck she doubles by wearing a pair of heavy gold earrings which have, over many years, stretched the cartilage. Her face and hands were weathered brown from the sun and hard work, but where her black trousers ruck up above her ankles ... her skin is as pink and smooth as the inside of a conch shell.*[xc]

Ah Bing has had a bad time with male relatives. Instead of working, they took to smoking opium, leaving the women folk to do labouring jobs as well as supporting the family. As a result, she is contemptuous of men. She is also well aware of the dire situation in China. Like other *amahs* from Hong Kong she makes the pilgrimage back to her village at Chinese New Year, dressed in layers of clothing, most of which she will leave behind. Travelling by train and bus from Kowloon, once in her local area, the rest of the journey will be undertaken on foot.

Meanwhile the Red Guards had broken into her family home and confiscated the paddy field where her family grew the rice on which they subsisted. Nor had their violence stopped at ransacking houses like theirs but they also destroyed the statutory and silk hangings in the local temples, a deliberate act of desecration. Monks and nuns were rounded up and paraded in the streets in ritual humiliation. Villagers were dragged out of their hiding places to witness these grotesque, public spectacles. The entire way of life that Ah Bing had been brought up with was being brought to a sudden, bloody end. Although she harboured some bitterness, Ah Bing was also stoical: the Fates had decreed these experiences for one and all. She prayed that Kuan Yin, the Goddess of Compassion, observing the horrors and woes of the world, would protect her from the ghosts that would emerge from the bodies floating into Hong Kong waters.

The core of Greenway's narrative is the search for identity by the two sisters of very different character in the exotic but disturbed setting of Hong Kong in 1967. Frankie, the eldest is something of a tomboy, a risk taker, and teenager determined to break with all the conventions which she feels inhibit her. She is also at the stage of becoming sexually aware: not only does she flirt with expatriate men who join the family on launch picnics and other outings but she leads on a deaf Chinese boy who is a schoolmate and who is keen on her. Meanwhile her sister, being altogether shyer and reserved, looks on.

One or two of the expatriate community are unconventional figures. Miss Tipley, a Chinese scholar fluent in Mandarin, is described by Ah Bing as '*daifu*', namely a lesbian. The deaf Chinese boy befriended by Frankie confirms this since his mother knew Miss Tipley in Shanghai where she was always known as 'uncle'. The Chinese seemed quite unperturbed by her sexual orientation, something she has to be discreet about in the Hong Kong circles in which she moves. Miss Tipley lives in a grand, colonial style on the Peak. Her house is perched on the edge of the 'jungle' or dense greenery of the mountain slope, equipped with capacious swimming pool. The city throbs below.

*Its packed apartment blocks, its busy harbour streaked with boats and white waves, are framed by a balustrade dotted with pink coral plants. And across the water, Kowloon with its quarried hills, planes landing regularly on the runways at Kai Tak. Ferns and St John's lily drip down the mould-streaked rocky cliff out of which the flat garden was carved.*[xci]

Her guests gather around the pool over afternoon tea; at these events 'English voices cascade across the garden, loud, commanding and authoritative'. [xcii]The guests include the wives of the Vice Chancellor of Hong Kong University and those of the *taipans* who run Jardine Matheson, always prominent in the gatherings of the great and good. While they chatter about the threat from China, Frankie jumps in the pool accompanied by the Chinese boy. Her thin wet, cotton shirt clings tightly to her dark nipples. Their flirtation continues.

One day the sisters get into trouble. As ever, led by Frankie and without Ah Bing's knowledge, they have escaped out of the house to witness a demonstration which turns into a confrontation between the Red Guards and the police. As they watch the girls are hustled away by two men who drag them into a stiflingly hot building nearby. Holding Frankie as hostage, they instruct her sister to carry a bag of lychees, laced with explosives, to the pier where the police boat is tied up and tell her to plant it there. If she does not comply, they will harm Frankie. Alice makes her way nervously down the street but cannot reach the pier which is cordoned off. Seeing an empty metal can, she deposits the parcel in it and retreats. Soon a great explosion rocks the stall nearby; a woman is killed and a boy badly injured. But the men holding Frankie have fled so the sisters can make their escape. The death and injuries she has caused haunt Alice for the rest of her time in Hong Kong.

An even greater tragedy awaits the family. While on a launch picnic in Middle Bay, they hear the approaching noise of a motor boat. It is the girls' father, back on leave. As the boat gets nearer and Frankie sees that it is indeed steered by her father. In great excitement she leaps off the launch to swim over to the boat so that she can be the first to jump into his arms. But disaster follows. Her father's boat is much nearer than she has realised; she hits the edge, gashing her head and is instantly killed. Diving into to rescue her, her father surfaces clutching her dead body. The family will never recover from this horror. Still in deep shock, they leave Hong Kong for good shortly afterwards.

The setting of the *White Ghost Girls* is the Hong Kong we have become familiar with. From dragon boat races to Buddhist temple ceremonies; the European architecture of St John's Cathedral and the Victorian redbrick of the University, the recognisable background is constantly and graphically evoked as the girls continue their growing up experiences. The world they move in is the typical mix of Chinese street life and the colonial bubble in which expatriates live. There is a strong sense throughout the narrative that the girls prefer the former and dislike the overbearing atmosphere of the latter. Frankie, in particular, is bent on adventure outside the constraints of a conventional life at home.

The most engaging character in the story is Ah Bing, the *amah*. She is practical and sensible, feeds stray cats and is the mainstay of the family home. Nor will she be taken for a fool: if challenged by anyone, she can respond in the most voluble Cantonese. Like many *amahs* she becomes a surrogate mother, closer to the girl's everyday life than their parents are. In that role she has tried her best to look after the girls and protect them but she realises that Frankie is an independent, uncontrollable spirit, with a will of her own. And Ah Bing's own experience has taught her that the twists and turns of fortune cannot be predicted. Her life has not been an easy one, she has witnessed destruction in the village she has come from on the mainland and hardship arriving in Hong Kong and needing to find work. When the girls go outside of the house on their own, they are in real danger. Ah Bing has the last word on Frankie's tragic end:

*American girls have everything. Po! Bad things happen even in rich families. Best to feed her now. Pray to Kuan Yin to look after her. Even naughty children need looking after.*[xciii]

# Chapter 10
# A Change of Flag: Christopher New

Christopher New is undoubtedly a cosmopolitan voice. English-educated he has spent much of his life in the East where for several decades from 1969 he was head of the department of philosophy at Hong Kong University. That academic background – during which time he published a book on philosophy and articles in learned journals – hid the inner novelist that was his true calling. Many of his stories are in Eastern settings. He himself explained that he thought too many Western writers were cocooned in their own world, believing that Europe and its culture was the centre of the universe. He was determined not to fall into that trap. As well as his celebrated trilogy on the apogee and decline of the British Empire in the East – *Shanghai* (1985)*, The Chinese Box* (1985) *and A Change of Flag* (1990), some of his novels were set elsewhere in the East, for example in India during the British Raj. For him the cliché about East is East and West is West is a parochial and tedious limitation on a creative writer's talent to cross boundaries and portray life in societies with different cultural norms.

*The Chinese Box* is set at the height of the Maoist Cultural Revolution on the mainland with its direct reverberations in Hong Kong as we have seen in Alice Greenway's *White Ghost Girls*. There were daily incidents involving bombs going off, skirmishes on the border with China and the sudden appearance of corpses in the harbour and on the beaches. The threat of invasion hung over the colony. Gangs of pro-Communist youths roamed the streets chanting from the Red Book causing roadblocks to be set up everywhere. There were daily battles with the police. These incidents are recorded in news story in the form of extracts from official sources, interrupting the flow of the narrative.

The hero of the story is Dimitri, a half-English and half-Russian academic who was born in Hong Kong and has fluent command of Cantonese which, to a certain extent, marks him out as a local boy. A *gweilo* or foreign devil speaking

Chinese provokes both respect and amusement among those who hear him. His upbringing in Hong Kong had been far from conventional. In a small flat overlooking her dress shop, his eccentric and flamboyant mother entertained fellow émigrés including Russian Jews who, like Solomon Bard, had arrived in the colony from Harbin and Shanghai when civil war was raging in China. Over a samovar, with an old fan whirling in the ceiling, they smoked, gossiped and drank tea.

From this exotic background Dimitri's marriage to Helen, a failed would-be concert pianist from England, was probably doomed from the start. When the narrative begins, their marriage is already in tatters. They have descended into daily wrangles, with an underlying feeling of despair. Their two children seem to be the only reason for their staying together. Meanwhile Dimitri has taken up with Julie, a Chinese bar girl observing somewhat ironically that:

*The mutual impenetrability of Chinese and Europeans in Hong Kong was nowhere denser than among the middle classes. Julie, a fisherman's daughter from a remote, outlying island, felt no gap between east and west at all. Western education seemed to create, or at least widen, the gap rather than narrow it. Perhaps because it weakened confidence in the existing culture, the native self.*[xciv]

Julie is sexually enticing with her delicate, Oriental body. Her straightforward acceptance of Dimitri is natural and relaxing in the way we have seen Suzie's attachment is to Robert in *The World of Suzie Wong*. Dimitri's easy-going rendezvous with her are in sharp contrast to the stilted atmosphere he faces at home where his only ally is Ah Wong, the *amah*, who can barely hide her disdain for Helen. While he can indulge in this dalliance without any qualms, for Julie the situation is quite different. Seeing her in the company of a *gweilo*, the Chinese would always assume she was a prostitute since no self-respecting Chinese woman would want to consort with a foreigner. Julie knows that but it does not seem to bother her, at least outwardly. In any case her liaison with Dimitri is the best she can expect given her outcast status.

Meanwhile expatriate life continues apparently unaffected by the daily turmoil on the streets. At a party on the Peak given by Jan, something of a mentor, Dimitri meets Mila Chan. Her background is very different from Julie's. She belongs to the Westernised group of middle-class Chinese. She is a professional dancer who has spent time in London but has hopes of continuing her career there as opportunities in Hong Kong are few and far between. Dimitri is at once taken by her physically; his first impression develops into an obsession with her lithe body and her sensuous lips. Moreover, he begins to appreciate her maturity and see her as a partner in a way that Julie, limited by her background, cannot realistically ever be.

With these extra-mural preoccupations on his mind, Dimitri cannot concentrate on his job at the university. An article, unfinished for months, lies on his desk. He barely follows proceedings of the committee on which he sits examining the case for allowing students who have failed examinations the chance to re-sit them. He spends time staring out of his study window:

*at the stone courtyard and the branches of the magnolia tree overspreading the little pond. Above and behind its thick green leaves, the top of the clock tower jutted out from the great hall, a strangely harmonious combination of gothic red-brick and vaguely Eastern architecture.*[xcv]

Outside the walls of the ivory tower of the university the riots and disturbances continue. Some demonstrators merely brandish the Little Red Book and chant revolutionary slogans. Others who are rounded up are reported as carrying knives, clubs and even home-made bombs. Large scale arrests take place on a daily basis. In several incidents protestors are shot dead by the police when they resist the order to disperse. There are incidents at the border with China. In one case a man who had publicly denounced Chairman Mao was riding his bicycle near the edge of Hong Kong territory. Suddenly a gang of four men rushed out and dragged him away before the police had time to intervene. When Dimitri and Mila make a trio to the New Territories, they observe the Gurkha troops near Lok Ma Chau digging up and sandbagging machine gun nests in preparations for an attack.

News comes of an escalation of violence in China itself; the British Embassy in Peking is attacked and burnt down. No one is sure of what the next stage in the political turmoil will be and the threat of invasion hangs over like a black cloud. Refugees who continue to flood into Hong Kong, despite the disturbances on its streets, bring harrowing tales of the Red Guards rampaging through towns and villages dragging people away without any rhyme or reason other than a vague suspicion that they are pro-Western, bourgeois types.

Dimitri gets caught up in a tangle over a terrorist incident in Central. He and Mila are driving along Des Voeux Road when they are held up at a police roadblock. While they wait in the car, they witness the police dragging along a demonstrator and pushing him into their van. A European police inspector is in charge with a Chinese corporal assisting him. From within the van Dimitri and Mila hear muffled screams and the thudding sound of beatings. Dimitri is aghast at this brutal, police treatment and decides to make an official complaint. In his witness statement he details all he has seen:

*I observed the inspector draw his revolver and the corporal kick the young man as he climbed the steps into the van. I heard sounds which appeared to be that of striking and hitting coming from the van. I heard a voice in Cantonese say "Put the boot in again." I heard some cries of pain.*[xcvi]

However, in her statement Mila avoids taking up a position and says she could not see or hear anything. She tells Dimitri afterwards that she has done this because if she gets implicated in an anti-corruption complaint, she will never get a visa to return to London to continue her dancing career. Months later when the case comes up in the court, she changes her evidence and corroborates Dimitri's account leading to the conviction of the policemen involved. However, that sentence is quashed in the appeal court.

Meanwhile life does not improve for Dimitri. Learning of his liaison with Mila, Helen commits suicide, leaving a desperate note wishing him well. At the same time Mila then tells him that she intends to return permanently to Shanghai having been offered a chance to dance there. There is a suggestion that changing her evidence to blacken the Hong Kong police has earned her the opportunity to return to China.

New is not shy of hinting at corruption and conspiracy in his narrative. Everyone is implicated, whether the top Chinese businessmen or the cadre of colonial servants. The businessmen are obsessive money-makers who want nothing to stand in their way. Rocking the boat is as unacceptable to them as it is to the colonial authorities who regard Dimitri's actions against police officers as close to treason.

Those not in business, like Dimitri's university colleague CK, are caught in the middle in the same way as families like the Chens in Janice Lee's *The Piano Teacher*. The Chens lead the high life, entertain expatriates at lavish receptions in their palatial home but are not really accepted by their own people. They have become too westernised in their behaviour. In many cases these upper-class Chinese have been educated abroad. CK is no exception having studied in America. He explains to Dimitri:

*But now I am half Westernised. Like most people in Hong Kong. They do not think we are proper Chinese anymore, in China. Neither one thing nor the other. Not fish nor fowl, you say?[xcvii]*

The turmoil of 1967 posed the greatest threat to Hong Kong's security since the Communist Revolution of 1949. In a certain sense its anarchic character made it even more of a threat than having a disciplined Red Army stationed at the border. In the event the worst fear, of an invasion, never materialized but events cast a shadow over life in the colony, adding a certain frenzy to the atmosphere.

Many of the familiar landmarks of Hong Kong are to be found in New's narrative – the Peak in its splendid isolation, the troubled backstreets of Kowloon, the idyllic slopes of Pokfulam and the nearby beaches at Repulse Bay and Stanley. In the outlying islands the fishing villages seem totally unchanged and unaffected by the upheavals in the city. The harbour still bustles with ships; the star ferry plies its way back and forth undisturbed. Hakka lady hawkers, wilful *amahs* and smiling Aberdeen fishing people are in the cast of characters in *The Chinese Box.* When Dimitri and Mila make the usual lovers' escape to Macau, we also encounter the well-known landmarks: the Praia Grande, the Camões Grotto, the English Protestant Cemetery. Like so many visitors from Hong Kong they enjoy the sleepy tranquillity they find there.

In *A Change of Flag,* we move twenty years on to the mid nineteen-eighties, another period of uncertainty though not of immediate military threat. This time the tension arose from the long-drawn out negotiations between Britain and China about the exact conditions of the impending hand-over in 1997. Constant rumours about Beijing's intransigence and demands at a time when Britain had little bargaining power unsettled entrepreneurs and the markets. Some business leaders who had themselves fled from China and feared a clampdown, moved their assets out of the colony. Many of the top Chinese echelon had already invested in foreign passports unsure whether the Hong Kong they knew would continue in the same way or whether it was finally finished as a capitalist entrepot and free-market. All the characters in this densely-written novel feel the shadow of this uncertainty hanging over them but they react to it in different ways.

The various themes of New's stories are woven around the lives and loves of the Johnston and Denton families whom we have met in *The Chinese Box*. Dimitri is still teaching at the university, more sardonic than ever. Alex and Elena, the children from his marriage with Helen, are now grown up although Elena behaves like an over-indulged teenager who seems entirely wrapped up in her own world of pleasure-seeking with a number of men but principally with Tom, a somewhat dissolute American journalist. Meanwhile Mila, Dimitri's former mistress and the reason for Helen's suicide when she discovered their relationship, has become his wife having escaped from the trauma of the Cultural Revolution in China. Her experiences there have left a mark on her character. She retains her dignity but has become taciturn and introverted, expecting the worst to happen at any moment.

The tangled web of the families' lives is seen through new eyes as Rachel, an American student who hopes to be supervised by Dimitri, gets to know them. She is unsure of the different customs of Europeans and Chinese, made more complicated by the Eurasian mix of the families. Mila, Dimitri's wife and Grace, Michael's wife, preserve a Chinese reticence, preferring not to show any outward signs of emotion. Preserving harmony is as important to them as telling the truth. At Helen's funeral the only person who showed any real grief is Ah Wong, the *amah*, who despite having had endless clashes with her 'missy', openly weeps for her. Ah Wong is in fact one of the most well-drawn characters in New's narrative. She:

*cleaned the Johnstons' house, washed, shopped and cooked with tireless care and pride. Every morning she swept the fallen leaves from the courtyard and steps, and the swishing scrape of bristles over stone was often the first sound Dimitri heard when he woke.*[xcviii]

Ah Wong, the daughter of a fisherman, is illiterate but not without her sense of place. When a stray cat is adopted by the family, she refuses to empty its litter tray, something that Elena has to do each day. Only when she has made her point, does Ah Wong change her attitude, in fact becoming the cat's main protector and friend. In her time, Helen had told Dimitri a number of times that it was no use trying to win in any battle with Ah Wong – the defeat over the litter tray reminds

Dimitri of guerrilla skirmishes in a war; domineering servants in the kitchen exact a lasting revenge for their country's submissions on the battlefield.

While Ah Wong's own room is a mess, she is generous to any relative wanting to stay with her. The only decoration she has are some plants which grow along the wall near her door. She is happiest when the house is full, with the children making a noise, even though it means more work for her. She finds Rachel too quiet and well-behaved. Ah Wong has been with the Johnstons ever since Elena was a baby deciding to take the job immediately at her interview with Helen even though she senses that her mistress has a difficult personality. Like all Hong Kong *amahs* she made the pilgrimage to the mainland at Chinese New Year.

*Dressed in her best black tunic and trousers she was setting out for China, carrying two enormous bundles almost as big as herself, full of toys and clothes for her brother's and sister's children, who would line up to greet her and thank her, and silently, invidiously, compare the value of their presents.*[xcix]

While Ah Wong was away the family cat disappeared. When she returned, exhausted from her trip, she was the person in the household most upset about what has happened. For a week or more at the cat's feeding time, she went out into the courtyard banging her enamel plate with a spoon. During the day time she walked around the entire district searching for the cat but without any luck.

News portrayal of Ah Wong is one of the strong points of his novel. *Amahs* have appeared in the background to many of the stories we have considered: in Alice Greenway's novel Ah Bing is a central character, but they are seldom portrayed as vividly as Ah Wong. Her combination of stubbornness, even cantankerousness, is matched by a strong sense of duty and an absolute loyalty to the Johnston family. Her stock, of Kwantung peasantry, was the backbone of domestic Hong Kong throughout its colonial history.

The other central character in the story is Patrick, Michael Denton's nephew. His is the most extended treatment of a gay character in our collected literature. From the very start we suspect that his flamboyance and bonhomie are a cover up. In public he poses in his English blazer, sporting extravagant Edwardian mannerisms. He sails through his academic duties at the university – where he is a colleague of Dimitri – with an eccentric light-heartedness, often forgetting to turn up to his supervisory appointments with Rachel. After several of his non-appearances, she decides to track him down at his own home. When she arrives there, she finds him with Chung Yan, a young man wearing tight black trousers and flicking his hair back from his eyes in a feminine gesture. Patrick is ill at ease at being found with Chung Yan; after a brief introduction he sends him on his way.

Noticing a pi-pa on the table, Rachel asks Patrick to give a recital.

*He began to play, sitting half-turned away from her, gazing over the balcony, only occasionally glancing down to watch where he placed his fingers. In his long gown and Chinese slippers, he reminded her still more now of one of those black and white photos you sometimes saw of Chinese intellectuals in the twenties.[c]*

The flat was decorated with scrolls and precious Chinese objects were on display adding to the effect of a Mandarin's retreat. In a bold, even brash moment, Rachel confronts Patrick about his sexuality. At first taken aback, he tells her that while camp behaviour is acceptable, to proclaim one's homosexuality in Hong Kong is unacceptable and given the existing law, can have serious consequences, including imprisonment. Even educated, university colleagues are deeply homophobic: one of them, Professor Cheung, has assured Patrick that all such deviant behaviour will be eliminated when China takes over the colony.

As the bond between Patrick and Rachel grows, he becomes more confident in letting her into his private life. One evening he suggests an excursion to a gay club which he assures her she will find different from any other of the segregated clubs in the colony. They take a taxi from his flat in mid-levels down to Wanchai, with its seedy night clubs and dance halls. In a dingy side-street Patrick leads Rachel up a dark staircase and raps loudly on a closed door. The waiters at entrance smile when they see him through the eye-hole but are less keen when opening the door, they find a woman with him. However, after murmurings, the pair are admitted. When her eyes get used to the dark, Rachel sees that everyone in the room – at the small tables, on the dance floor or at the bar – are men. They are usually in pairs – Chinese with Chinese, Europeans with Europeans and mixed-race couples. Patrick tells Rachel that among the latter, the Europeans are known as 'rice queens' and the Chinese boys with them as 'potato queens'. After only a short while, Rachel has had enough while Patrick is much put out by seeing Chung Yan with another European man across the floor. They quickly take their leave.

The dénouement of the novel is a frightening scene in Patrick's flat. While he is cavorting with Chung Yan in the bedroom, a gang of four triad members burst into the flat. They threaten Patrick with knives unless he will cooperate by simulating anal sex with Kwan Yun while they take photographs which will be used to blackmail him. Patrick is forced to go through with their demand. When they have finished, they disappear and with them Chung Yan whom he is never to see again. The ransom demand is exorbitant; Patrick is desperate and has to seek financial help from his uncle, Michael.

Michael sees it as another family duty and gets the money for Patrick. A meeting is arranged for Patrick to meet the triads in a canteen but there is another shock awaiting him. A different gang of thugs burst in and there is a bloody confrontation between the rival groups with the death of one of the canteen staff. Some of the triads are captured by the police who arrive rapidly on the scene; Patrick will be a star witness in their trial. But in taking that part, the entire story of his involvement will become public. He cannot face it and commits suicide by jumping off his balcony. Meanwhile, Michael is charged over his illegal dealings in getting Lily out of China.

The New's dramatic story is very much set in a modern, changing Hong Kong. Although some of the usual colonial trappings are there – the Peak, the hotel lobbies and the ever-influential *amahs*, the mood has shifted from *dim sum* to *burgers*. But the street scenes have not changed. As one of his characters wanders through Temple Street:

*The stalls, close-packed beneath their incandescent glaring lamps, were still crowded, the hawkers sweating in their singlets as they bargained, wrapped and gave change... He liked the noise, the closeness of the people, the steamy smells of cooked-food stalls, the songs of the kerbside opera-singers and the blind musicians, even the dead smiles of the old tarts loitering by the park.[ci]*

There is also a continual reminder of the seamier sides of the city. Rat bins left from the time of the plague are still used in filthy backstreets, littered with garbage. In areas like North Point there are bleak apartment blocks, with endless dark corridors, rabbit-warren rooms shared by dozens of people and windows locked and barred which face equally grim concrete buildings. In Sai Yin Poon, a stone's throw from the upmarket Central district, there are crumbling buildings perched up narrow, old streets. An air of decay hangs over everything. It is a far cry from life on the Peak or the smart hotel lounges.

Patrick and Rachel's visit to the gay bar is the most explicit portrayal of the evolving gay scene in 1980s Hong Kong. This is a cosmopolitan city influenced by developments across the world, bringing previously entirely hidden behaviour out in the open. Gay bars in Lan Kwai Fong now operated openly instead of being hidden in dark backstreets in Wanchai. The clientele was a mix of westerners and Chinese. Some people were shocked by these developments, whether conservative members of the expatriate community or the traditional Chinese hierarchy as Xu Xi explores in *Hong Kong Rose.* Nevertheless, the sub-culture is left to flourish undisturbed by the authorities, another example of the laissez-faire administration of the colony.

At the same time old distinctions among the Chinese themselves persist. Newly-arrived northerners are all dubbed 'Shanghainese' by the locals wherever they originate from. They are not trusted, particularly if they do not speak Cantonese. If they are successful in enriching themselves that causes resentment among the locals who consider that they should be the first to benefit from the new prosperity. From the northerner's point of view, the 'slippery' Cantonese cannot be trusted. They seem willing to change sides and are too deferential to their British overlords. But underlying these differences, New explores an essential 'Chineseness' which they all share, however Westernised they appear to be on the surface. The locals never feel entirely comfortable in the expatriate community no matter how much they seem to be part of the social elite. They retain traditional Chinese values, such as the family network, and hanker after recognition in the motherland even while rejecting political developments there. Whatever hardship and horror have come about in China, there remains an underlying sense of patriotism.

The most strident expression of this inner, sometimes hidden identity is expressed by Lily. Even after her bitter experiences during confinement in the Cultural Revolution, she exclaims:

*I don't want to turn into a Briton. I'm still Chinese.*[cii]

It is a sentiment that echoes Han Suyin's of the 1950s.

# Chapter 11
# Good-Bye Hong Kong: Xu Xi

Xu Xi, now settled permanently in New York, once declared that she lived somewhere on the flight path between there and Hong Kong. Born of Chinese-Indonesian parents who came to settle in the colony in the nineteen-fifties, she went to school in Hong Kong before completing a university degree in the United States where she eventually obtained citizenship. She claims that not doing post-graduate work saved her as a novelist. Writing was always her passion from her early childhood days. Her chosen language has been English; she indeed became something of a champion of Asian writers using English as their medium of expression, though, as we shall see she had some reservations about her own dependency, as a writer, on using a non-Sinitic language.

For many years she combined writing with managerial jobs in the corporate sector, including in marketing, an unusual background for a writer of fiction. When she came to devote herself entirely to writing, Hong Kong featured prominently in her work, both as a local and a local made foreign. Her musings about her Chinese heritage take various forms, including articles and essays but most poignantly in her fiction. As a tribute to her Hong Kong heritage, she compiled an anthology of local writing from 1945 in prose and in verse. Success as a writer has led to prizes and distinctions for pieces published in journals and newspapers. Later she took up a teaching post in the Chinese university of Hong Kong until the programme she taught was unexpectedly closed down.

Much of her itinerant life, between Hong Kong and America, is reflected in her novels, *Hong Kong Rose* among them. Rose is a local girl, schooled at Maryknoll Convent. Like Xu Xi, she continues her education in the United States, returning to Hong Kong after various amorous adventures there to marry her girlhood sweetheart, Paul. From the freedom of her American life, she suddenly finds herself in a much more formal setting than she has been used to,

126

a formality of life for the upper class in Hong Kong that Xu Xi often highlights. That lifestyle, revolving around a small circuit of hotels, clubs and shopping malls, seems surreal and stage-like.

Once back in Hong Kong, Rose herself is once again entangled in the Chinese family matrix on the one hand and the privileged world of the Westerners, *gweilos*, on the other. The Westerners, most of who are in top corporate or professional jobs:

*all drew clear divisions between themselves and locals, and could even be quite snobbish and overbearing.*[ciii]

But xenophobic exclusion worked the other way as well: local Chinese discriminated against 'mongrel' interlopers like the westernised Rose as much as they did against foreigners and Eurasians. Nor did they welcome northerners from Shanghai prospering in what they regarded as their home territory.

The racial divide, segregating the different communities, is even more complicated because Paul, although looking entirely Chinese, is in fact Eurasian. Working as she does in an international environment, Rose, with her perfect English, finds herself as an intermediary between the Chinese and the foreign community. She is expected to understand the norms that underlie behaviour in these different camps and to adjust to each accordingly. In this respect Hong Kong of the 1970s has changed little: these social divisions are much the same as those in the 1950s of Austin Coates and Han Suyin. Only certain individuals, with some advantage of status conferred by education, profession or wealth, could cross the boundaries that divided the different communities.

In the background to Rose's growing up is her relationship with her twin sister, Regina, echoing that of the sisters in Alice Greenway's *White Ghost Girls*. Regina is a tomboy and a rebel who has strong opinions about everything and expresses them freely, whether palatable to those who hear them or not. She is an artist, leading a bohemian life in New York, masochistically attracted to men who exploit her, often leaving her in suicidal moods. She is entirely alienated from the Chinese family life she would be forced to lead in Hong Kong though her mother still dotes on her at the expense of affection for Rose. Despite the outward appearance of toughness, Regina is in fact more vulnerable than Rose. She is given to erratic mood swings and has violent dreams. One night in a frenzied nightmare she knocks over a ceramic vase, smashing it to pieces but appears to have no recollection of the incident the next day when Rose mentions it. Although Rose's goodwill will be tested by Regina's unruly behaviour, the bond between the sisters, forged in their childhood days, remains strong.

Rose's husband, Paul is a serious and successful lawyer who hides his bisexuality in a cloak of respectability. It is only after they are married and living in Hong Kong, that Rose discovers his homosexual side, something known to her parents-in-law but not spoken about. Nor does Rose tell her own parents about it: the loss of face of such a revelation would be too great for them to bear. As the months pass, Paul's behaviour becomes more and more erratic. He disappears for whole nights leaving Rose abandoned at their home, wondering when she will see him next. Eventually Rose discovers the existence of his male lover, one Man Kee, who has taken to calling her to deliver nasty messages and threats, jealous of her marital bond that Paul will not break. As a man, even with his homosexual orientation, Man Kee is protected in the patriarchal, Hong Kong society where women are subordinate creatures. He seems to be able to get away with behaviour that is so at odds with traditional Chinese family values. His attempt to drag Paul away from Rose would not only affect the couple but ruin the reputation of both families.

Meanwhile Rose herself, emotionally confused and needing a sexual outlet, has a series of affairs with different men, almost all Westerners. The most attractive of them is Elliot Cohen, a lively *gweilo* who has taken the trouble to learn Cantonese in order to beguile the ladies that he suits. Unlike other foreigners, he treats everyone as equals. Elliot's own family life in the States was chaotic, leading to public separation from his wife. Rose reflects that pretending that nothing untoward is happening in her own life at least saves that kind of exposure and humiliation. Nor is she fooled by the casual warmth and sincerity Elliot exudes in the American way, contrasting so strongly with what can be the somewhat stilted manner of Hong Kong people even when they are offering the hand of friendship.

The lovers meet on Thursdays, the day of the week when Paul disappears on his gay assignations. Their rendezvous must take place in private; any appearance in public would immediately be noticed in the small world of Hong Kong society. When the lovers find themselves together in New York they can cast aside their furtive meetings and spend more time together openly. Rose notices that Elliot's cool, business-like Hong Kong persona is thrown aside as he returns to his New York roots. He is suddenly more relaxed and direct, taking things as they come, enticing Rose to do the same. She ruminates:

*This wasn't the Elliot I knew in Hong Kong, restrained and overly formal for the most part, and almost shy in his politeness.*[civ]

For his part, Elliot cannot resist commenting on the hypocrisy in Rose's attitude. In Hong Kong she acts out her part in the Chinese traditional family while in his company, all her inhibitions vanish. In spite of his self-righteousness, Elliot is in fact still entangled in a relationship with his former lover, Leanna, a bond so strong that it eventually tears him away from Rose. The contrast between the cities, New York and Hong Kong, is used as a backcloth to showing different cultural behaviour: Elliot is relaxed in an American way in the Big Apple; Rose is uptight in outwardly prim and proper Hong Kong where everything unpleasant or ugly is hidden away and the most important thing is to save face. Each of them behaves differently in the two different cities. Nevertheless, in the relationship with Elliot, Rose seeks to assert herself as an individual, not subject to the suffocating constraints of the Chinese family web. In a role reversal, Elliot becomes her concubine, making up, to some extent, for the compromised married life she leads with Paul.

Leanna's revenge for Rose's intrusion into her long-standing affair with Elliott is to expose her relationship to Marion, Paul's mother, an influential figure in the narrative. Both of Paul's parents, while not condoning it, accept their son's homosexuality but seek to protect his marriage to Rose in spite of, or because of, it. In the conservative society of Hong Kong marriage was essential and such heterodox sexual proclivities had to be hidden as we have seen in Christopher New's portrayal of Patrick in *A Change of Flag.* Marion had become a surrogate mother for Rose supplanting her own, hysterical mother who despite everything, insists on favouring Regina over her, ignoring the latter's outrageous behaviour. In Rose's own family the most sympathetically portrayed person is her father, a gambler addicted to horse racing but one who maintains a stoical detachment from his wife's fits and starts. Nevertheless, like his wife he is keen that Rose and Paul should have children and as time goes by, his anxiety increases. Eventually Rose tells her father about Paul but he ignores what she has said. Rose concludes from his silence that:

*I couldn't overturn everything around me. My war, unlike his, hadn't ended yet. In my and my father's worlds, the forces of change were controlled from without, not within, and it was up to us to navigate as best we could, and trust that the winds would favor our path.[cv]*

The setting of this tangled web is unmistakeably the Hong Kong of its period. The urban landmarks – Lan Kwai Fong and its bars, Lane Crawford Department store, Jade Garden and tree-lined Nathan Road – are as recognisable as they were in the days of Martin Booth and Janice Lee although Xu Xi is less concerned than Booth with exploring the side-streets and back alleys. Instead, Rose enjoys the luxurious atmosphere at the Mandarin Hotel where society wives gathered for afternoon tea and business people met for drinks after work. By contrast there are occasional excursions on the bus – from Prince Edward Road to Tsim Sha Tsui; passing blocks of flats in Kowloon Tong, the setting, as we shall see for Paul Theroux's novel. The rural background of Austin Coates's New Territories is still there but is increasingly being urbanised by overspill from the city.

Something of the more peaceful side of Hong Kong is also captured. In the late autumn during the typhoon season when the nights are cooler and less humid, outdoor life becomes pleasant. Rose takes a boat trip to Sai Kung where the water is clean and crystal blue. She is reminded of a childhood excursion there with Regina who dived off the launch as soon as it was moored. Egged on by Elliot, Rose takes up the challenge to water ski and soon finds herself gliding along the translucent water. It is a far cry from the urban jungle.

Xu Xi's primary focus is on people, with all their complex identities rather than on their physical surroundings. Although Paul is Eurasian, his Chinese appearance saves him from having to choose one side or the other, a dilemma facing Eurasians whose appearance shows both ethnicities. But there is another trap for Rose to fall into, given her overseas background. While Paul insists, they are Chinese and cannot be anything else, Rose muses:

*Something about being our brand of overseas Chinese, mongrel Chinese – desperate on the one hand for the all-important deih waih, 'position' equal status actually with the supposedly 'real' Chinese of Hong Kong – made us hard but a brittle kind of hard.[cvi]*

Both Paul and Rose must cope with this complexity, he seeming more Chinese but with a sexual orientation that is unconventional; Rose outwardly westernised yet entrapped in an overbearing Chinese family web of obligations from which she accepts as her fate.

In the *Unwalled City* we move on several decades to 1995 when the looming handover of British rule to China in 1997, casts a shadow over everything. The metaphor of the 'unwalled city' is only made crystal clear at the end of the novel when Albert, an outwardly trendy, but characteristically inhibited Chinese friend, tells Vince, the expatriate American:

*Don't you see? Here in Hong Kong, we were never inside the wall. We're like barbarians. Mongols at bay.[cvii]*

Being outside the wall applies not only to Chinese who have Western connections but also to Eurasians who are discriminated against by both the Chinese and the expatriate communities. Gail Szeto, one of the characters in the novel is part of this *jaahpjung*, mixed, Eurasian community. She cannot escape from being labelled as an outsider, even though at certain angles, she might be physically mistaken for being Caucasian.

*Miscellaneous, assorted species. Jaahpjung. Not like anyone else, never belonging inside the species, at least, not the species as defined by the respectable, family obsessed Hong Hong yan, the 'real Chinese' the only 'humans' who counted.*

*In her dreams as a child she [Gail] lived outside the Great Wall, where she would knock and knock on the door to the Wall but no one would ever let her in.[cviii]*

The *Unwalled City* has a denser and a more multi-layered plot than *Hong Kong Rose* which makes it a more challenging read. This is because of the multiple characters involved and the to-and-fro of the narrative between them. The mood is of intense introspection as the protagonists, mostly female, struggle with their emotional responses to the world around them as well as with sexual desires that lead them into awkward tangles. Andanna, a model and a rather spoilt creature, chain smokes her way through various affairs; her background is one of privileged wealth although she chooses to lead a bohemian life centred on jazz with Michael, her partner. Although smitten with the Hong Kong fever for work, she is not financially dependent on it as her family belong to the Cantonese/Shanghainese plutocracy who runs all the colony's important businesses. That background enables her to indulge in her semi-bohemian life, flavoured by the latest quintessentially Hong Kong developments, such as Canto-pop music. Endless socializing takes place in coffee house and bars; alcohol and drugs are part of the culture round the sloping streets above Central.

At an opulent wedding reception, she meets Gail, immaculately coiffured and looking like a movie star, with her son Gu Kwan, a polite and precocious young boy of seven who addresses her in perfect Cantonese but speaks English just as well. Not only is Gail Eurasian but she is Harvard educated and thereby twice removed from the magic circle drawn by the Hong Kong Chinese community. Although she is a highly successful professional, usurping the position of a man by holding a top job in a bank, even that does not gain her admittance to local, Chinese society. Nor is her attempt to introduce greater informality at work successful. The Hong Kong employees she works with are used to a more formal relationship with the bosses and they prefer it. Gail's English is naturally as fluent as Gu Kwan's: Andanna thinks that if one had one's eyes closed one would not imagine they were not *gweilos,* so perfect were their accents. Gail's life is also a disturbed one, separated from Gu Kwan's father who seems to have no interest in his son's welfare.

Andanna has a close, if somewhat fraught friendship with Clio, an old school chum, with whom she should be able to be completely open but is held back, ironically, by Clio's forthrightness. When Andanna tries to avoid discussing her likely break-up with Michael, Clio persists, warning her that she will feel bereft when it actually happens. Clio is also not above telling Andanna that she is a spoilt, Hong Kong 'princess' who doesn't have to work at all because of her family's wealth. Her frankness, though it can be disconcerting, is nevertheless an important part of their friendship.

As her relationship with Michael comes to an end, Andanna becomes obsessed with Vince, an expatriate American with a complicated matrimonial past who leads an unconventional life as a photographer in Hong Kong. Vince has been through two marriages and finds himself back on the dating circle in Hong Kong, with the advantage that local girls are keen to hitch up with a foreigner. He has an ambiguous friendship with Albert, whom he suspects is gay. Albert is a slightly built, effeminate creature. Forthright and prepared to pronounce on any subject, Albert glosses over the subject of sex. He tells Vince that New York is *passé* compared to Hong Kong, with its vibrant future. He jokes about the political situation, unaffected by the forthcoming settlement of 'one country, two systems' as he has rights to residence in both.

*This strange friendship had its moments. Albert had a remarkable face. Unlined and smooth skinned. Hard to believe it belonged to someone who was almost fifty. Next to him Vince felt old.*[cix]

Like the others in their circle, they frequent spots like the Jazz Club in Lan Kwai Fong. After one of their late-night binges Vince is surprised to be invited back to Albert's place to share a joint. When he says that he doesn't even know where Albert lives, the address is scribbled on the back of a napkin. It is just round the corner from the Jazz Club, next to the gay bar whose customers spill onto the nearby pavements. Albert presses Vince to come even though it is well past midnight. The sequel of their rendezvous is never spelt out.

Another character in the tangled narrative is Colleen, a foreigner, who has an affair with Vince but remains tied to her husband, Kwok Po. She is in the entertainment business and anxious to promote Andanna's career, convinced that her physique and sexiness should get her to the top of that particular greasy pole. Colleen is convinced that the twenty first century would belong to China and Hong Kong people needed to understand that. More people in the world spoke Chinese than any other language: why did Chinese people need to learn English? She makes sure that she herself is conversant in both Mandarin and Cantonese. Nevertheless, she is most at home in Hong Kong.

The physical background to this claustrophobic world is the usual Hong Kong hotspots: The Mandarin and Excelsior hotels, the bar at the Hyatt; the raucous mix to be found in Lan Kwai Fong where the heroines of the story can be found cavorting into the early hours on most weekends. It is a world in which everyone knows each other and cannot avoid meeting one another in their regular haunts. Some modernisation has taken place in this familiar setting, everyone carries cell phones and Canto-pop has become the rage, nouveau Asian cuisine has replaced homely, Cantonese cooking. But the social behaviour of the characters in the narrative – the anxiety of Eurasians, the Chinese cover up of illicit sex, the obsessive pursuit of wealth – all echo the Hong Kong of Austin Coates, Han Suyin and Timothy Mo.

The immediate political background of the handover in 1997 is in the air but does not seem to interfere with the molly-coddled life of Andanna and her circle. Occasional comparisons are made with other cities – some of the scenes are set in Singapore where the atmosphere is far less frenzied and more controlled. Colleen, finding herself there, enjoys the calm ceremony of afternoon tea when the rain has cooled everything down. One of the changes in Hong Kong is the increasing use of Mandarin which Albert, who mixes with influential mainlanders speaks perfectly but Albert is a survivor ready to adapt to any unexpected situation as it arises. His view is that as the sun sets on the British Empire, it rises in China, gradually becoming an economic giant on the world stage. On the other hand, Colleen's husband, Kwok Po, mixes up the two types of Chinese in a 'Chinglish' dialect.

Xu Xi's final word on Hong Kong appears as a memoir, *Dear Hong Kong* (2017) written in an elegiac tone. She begins with the declaration that she has 'already begun to say goodbye to my city' as she contemplates the future and the end of the transitional period agreed between Britain and China. Then she develops the theme that her relationship to the city is one of a lover, now about to lose her loved one:

*Dear Hong Kong, I had not planned on saying goodbye. Not yet. We were going to have many more years together, our love affair peaking and valley-ing as it has, as it does... oh, I knew I would leave you one day, when age caught up to my transnational life and it would no longer be possible to embrace such an immovably petulant, albeit persistent lover.*[cx]

As usual when a love affair comes to an end, the fault seldom lies only on one side. Xu Xi, on her various trips back to the city has been complaining about changes, about a deterioration that affects every aspect of life in the 'unwalled city'. Some of the changes are the result of globalisation. In Lan Kwai Fong everyone is eating sushi or moussaka or vindaloo and listening to jazz instead of Chinese opera. Technology has not helped. While for Xu Xi and her generation, literature reminded one of one's humanity; in the new world of instant communication, young people are constantly bombarded with bad news. And to make matters worse the young are told, by their leaders that they do not understand the city's problems and should leave it to their elders and betters to sort things out.

At the same time everyone, young and old, is aware that China is peeking out from behind the bamboo curtain and beginning to interfere more directly in Hong Kong affairs. Unease at that development combined with general discontent about the cost of living and the influx of unwelcome, wealthy mainlanders led to the yellow umbrella movement with occupation of central parts of the city by its organisers, not entirely appreciated by the older generation who remembered that things were not always rosy in 'the good old days'. Nor are businesses and shop keepers pleased that they have to close up during the street disturbances. Hong Kong does not present a united front.

Xu Xi herself is not under the illusion that everything in the past was rosy. Her own family experience, of moving from a well-situated apartment with harbour view in downtown Tsim Sha Shui to a flat in Kowloon Tong when she was still a schoolgirl, made her keenly aware of how unaffordable spacious living had become in desirable, central districts. Even so that experience seemed a bourgeois problem compared to the hardship which some of her fellow pupils had to endure, returning to tiny apartments to help their parents earn a living through a variety of cottage industries.

Other aspects of Hong Kong life have never been to her taste. The obsession with making money had led to a closed society, without wider expression and untrammelled creativity:

*Profit is not a sufficient motivation for the human condition even though it does provide impetus for many especially in HK.*[cxi]

Moreover, Xu Xi herself had had to leave Hong Kong to become a writer. She believes that if she had stayed there, in her airline job, she would have no doubt risen through the ranks of the organisation. She might even have produced a vanity book in her retirement. Instead in the eleven years of her exile, she became an established writer.

The education system had not been brilliant. The standard of English which she encountered as a university teacher showed the poor quality of this legacy. Mention of English leads her to speculate on why she chooses to write in the language at all, wondering if this makes her a traitor to her native Chinese ethnicity. This is a complicated matter which she had written about in an article entitled 'Why I stopped being Chinese' a few years earlier. She begins by rehearsing her Indonesian-Chinese heritage. Her father, a Mandarin speaker, never acclimatises to Cantonese when they move to Hong Kong. A musical man he regards Cantonese as coarse, guttural and atonal. He forbids its use at home. Xu Xi herself, saying that she sounds more fluent in it than she actually is, likes its guttural directness. Fortunately, her fluency in both Chinese languages (and Cantonese is a language not a dialect) saves her from the embarrassment of speaking 'Chinglish' which muddles them together as we have seen in her fictional characters.

Her choice of English as her language of expression is also a Hong Kong choice, a freedom hardly imaginable in the motherland, China, where every effort is being made to tempt overseas people, pining for their home village, back by promising a brighter, better future. But adopting English as the main medium of her work as a writer, she has suffered continuous discrimination. A Taiwanese acquaintance also living in the United States, criticises her adaptation to American life. Yet the critical, shrill lady and her family, are entirely rooted in New Jersey, seldom making visits to their 'ancestral home' unlike Xu Xi who has spent extended years in Hong Kong and has a deep knowledge of Chinese culture, particularly its literature. It is rank hypocrisy. However, because Xu Xi's accent is not as pure as hers, her critic says she is not 'real Chinese'. Xu Xi observes:

*Yet her attitude was not uncommon. All my life I have encountered ethnic Chinese who deny me the right to be Chinese, because of my language, demeanour, blood.*[cxii]

Even in Hong Kong, Xu Xi is officially categorised as a foreigner, although one with a permanent right of abode, as neither parent was born on Chinese soil. Friends in Hong Kong, who should know better, are surprised that she is familiar with unusual dishes, cuisine being regarded as something only locals can really know about. But despite all that, the farewell with 'her city' is painful.

Like other post-colonial writers Xu Xi struggles to understand why she should write in English. There is a good reason: literature must be universal and English is the *lingua franca* of the international reading public. Moreover, it has been her major medium of expression all through her life. While she can read Chinese without difficulty and express herself orally in both in Cantonese and Mandarin, her writing voice has to be heard in English. She cannot know whom or what she betrays by using it and cannot accept that a writer is or is not Chinese.

Life as a Chinese in the outside world is too complicated; complexity is a term loved in the Chinese language for all its doubling, repetitive, overlapping effect.

There is only one conclusion:

*Here is the moment of surrender: I must stop being Chinese. As you [the reader] can see for yourself, it is just too complicated.*[cxiii]

Her final words to her 'lover' is dramatic enough:

*Dear HK. I'm breaking things off. May fortune always shine upon you.*[cxiv]

# Chapter 12
# Fragrant Harbour: John Lanchester

John Lanchester is a prolific writer: journalist, essayist, and novelist; he is as well known for his non-fiction work as for his fiction. He was brought up in Hong Kong in the 1960s, returning to school in England and later studying at Oxford. As a journalist he wrote for most of the leading British newspapers, including the *Guardian* and the *Daily Telegraph*, but he also contributed to the *London Review of Books* and the *New York Review of Books*. His first novel, *The Debt to Pleasure* about a sybaritic Englishman, won him both the Whitbread Book Award in 1996 and a year later, the Hawthorden Prize. A second novel, *Mr Phillips* followed in 2000. In 2002, Lanchester returned to his Hong Kong roots with *Fragrant Harbour*. His latest novel, *The Wall*, has been named on the Booker Prize long list.

*Fragrant Harbour* is set in the Hong Kong of the 1980s although the chief protagonist, Tom Stewart has lived in the colony since the 1930s when the narrative begins. The other two principal characters are Sister Maria and Matthew Ho, the latter a Chinese refugee who turns out to be Tom Stewart's grandson.

On board ship sailing for Hong Kong, Tom Stewart takes Cantonese lessons from Sister Maria, a fellow passenger and nun who is travelling back to China, so that he can manage at least the rudiments of the language before his arrival. She is a strict teacher, providing him with vocabulary cards and teaching him the monosyllabic language. The couple, watched over by Sister Benedict, get on well: it is the beginning of a great romance.

Once in Hong Kong, Tom sets up the *Empire Hotel* on the shaded, tree-lined Nathan Road. This is residential, calm Kowloon of pre-war days. Hong Kong is altogether a much emptier place: crossing on the Star Ferry, Tom sees the island like a rock on which people have camped rather than as a cramped city of skyscrapers it was to become. Before long the hotel itself soon becomes an oasis for locals who prop up the bar and make the usual expatriate complaints about the climate and servants while a sturdy, turbaned Sikh, with a shotgun, guards the entrance. There is much talk about the turmoil in China and whether it will spill over to the colony although that threat seems to have little effect on the style of expatriate life. Meanwhile a regular stream of international business travellers provides a lucrative income for Tom.

Like other new arrivals Tom enjoys the exotic sights that greet him on the streets:

*Hakka women in their sombreros, which smelt of oil or lacquer; coolies dragging impossible bundles on their backs; rickshaw men, gold-toothed shoe shiners, gap-toothed Japanese businessmen, opium smokers visible through side-street windows, eagles circling wind currents on the Peak, the brake man's crisp uniform on the Peak tram and the view from the Peak towards Kowloon...*[cxv]

On Sunday afternoons there is a mad clattering noise of mahjong coming from the servants' quarters; there is Chinese art to absorb, the cult of *fung shui* to understand; dragon boat races to watch. All this adds to the vivid and alluring atmosphere of the city.

Soon Tom learns of the various Chinese festivals including that of the Hungry Ghosts when it is obligatory to clean the graves of ancestors. He enjoys entering temples choking with the fumes of smoking joss sticks, Gods and guardian painted in blazing colours. Then there is the endless celebration of food; the serving of meals in refined ceramic bowls.

But what surprises Tom most is the expatriate side of Hong Kong life. The need to conform seemed to be overwhelming, something he had already had a taste of, on the P & O ship which brought him to the East. Not only were there intricate hierarchies in the government service but in the great merchant houses, the *hongs*, there were complicated codes of behaviour, baffling to any outsider. In the social venues of this society: the Jockey Club, the Yacht Club, the Hong Kong Club itself:

*It was P & O all over again, but more so. The whole idea of coming East was to loosen the shackles England imposed, it seemed to me – that was self-evident. If you so liked the way things were in England, why would you leave? But the sense of respectability, the need to conform and to fit, was crushing. There were codes, visible and invisible, everywhere.[cxvi]*

Each organisation or business had its own set of customs and practices with strict rules about what was acceptable behaviour and what was not. What one wore, who one talked to and what one said were strictly monitored. Not following the rules resulted in exclusion from one's own people.

One of the passing visitors at the hotel, one Wilfred Austen, no doubt meant to be W. H. Auden, remarks that the Chinese seem to be so much more intelligent than the expatriates, making it an embarrassment to be a white person. Nevertheless, the locals were relegated to an inferior position:

*The Chinese were not invisible, since not even the expatriate community could deny reality to that extent, but they were no more than extras – walk-on parts, menials, an exotic but ignored backdrop to the important real stage. Nothing to do with the Chinese was quite real.[cxvii]*

A few years after Tom had established the *Empire Hotel*, by then a flourishing business, war breaks out. What seemed like impregnable Hong Kong suddenly becomes indefensible as the Japanese destroyed the RAF aircraft on the ground and begin a land invasion through the New Territories.

Sister Maria has disappeared during the raids and Tom undertakes a desperate search for her in the New Territories even as the Japanese troops advance through the rural area towards Kowloon. Soon everyone is trapped, some hiding out longer like Trudy and her friends do on the Peak in Janice Lee's *Piano Teacher*. Tom is captured and with many others, interned in Stanley Prison. Chosen by one of the medical fraternities, Stanley at least offers an open space with fresh air. Tom discovers that even in these straitened conditions, the colonial pattern of life does not disappear, its civilian hierarchies duplicated in the unlikely surroundings of the prison camp. There are eccentric exceptions to social constraints: the gaunt, already skeletal Professor Cobb continues to give talks on poets of the Tang era, of which he is an expert, to any of his fellow prisoners who wish to attend.

After the war, Hong Kong makes a rapid recovery, boosted by becoming a strategic centre of operations in the Cold War. Increased American investment as well as a flood of entrepreneurial refugees from Shanghai adds to the boom.

Nevertheless, there is a big difference between the two cities: whereas in Shanghai most things, including prostitution and drug taking, are conducted fairly openly, in Hong Kong everything is secret and hidden:

*It's not that Hong Kong people would mind staying in a hotel which used to be a Chinese cathouse, but they would mind people thinking they didn't mind, because it would show they weren't respectable. So, it's no go.* [cxviii]

A cloak of respectability is draped over everything in order to save face, by far the most important consideration.

Tom returns to running the *Empire Hotel* which does so well that he is able to open a second establishment, more of a guest house, in the peaceful surrounds of Deep Water Bay. Sister Maria is back in Hong Kong but after being involved as a witness in a triad case, she disappears once more, resurfacing in Fujian province in China. There she bears a child, Tom's son which he only learns about much later. However, it is the stormy period of the Cultural Revolution; the family is attacked and almost everyone is killed, including Tom's son. The only survivor is Matthew, his grandson, who manages to escape the slaughter. He soon joins the streams of refugees making for Hong Kong through Guangzhou. He has with him the letter written by Sister Maria which proves his lineage. Like many fellow arrivals from the mainland, he finds lodgings in a poor area of Kowloon and must start to eke out a living. Knowing about Tom, he starts to shadow him from a distance but his Chinese reticence prevents him from approaching his grandfather straight away. He waits for the right moment to do so.

In the end, the meeting of grandfather and grandson takes place in the unlikely venue of a taxi queue. Matthew sees that Tom, as a *gweilo*, is being pushed aside by people behind him. He comes to the rescue, chasing off the locals who shamelessly try to jump the queue. However, he still does not reveal his identity at that point. It is only later that he eventually presents himself to Tom as his grandson. Tom is startled but delighted to discover his relationship with Matthew: their bond is sealed. Matthew is rescued from a life of penury and sent to university to study, supported by Tom who by this time has sold the *Empire Hotel* and has retired to a comfortable life in the more peaceful surrounds of his Deep Water Bay house.

Lanchester's novel, spanning as it does decades of Hong Kong's history, captures the ups and downs of the city's life with great poignancy. During the period of the narrative the three major crises points are the Japanese occupation from 1941, the Communist take-over in China in 1949 and the Cultural Revolution in the 1960s. Tom Stewart experiences the first of these, the most traumatic, as a prisoner in Stanley Camp. Young and in good health he survives the deprivations of internment until the end of the war, in 1946. In 1949 he is among the expatriates expecting a takeover of the colony at any moment. Yet with a vast influx of refugees, Hong Kong enters its post-war boom. The *Empire Hotel* flourishes during the period. In the 1960s he witnesses the street riots and disturbances, with Red Guard sympathisers rampaging the streets, as we have seen in Alice Greenway's *The White Ghost Girls*. No harm comes to him or to the business.

Yet throughout this time certain aspects of life in the increasingly crowded and frenetic city do not seem to change. The expatriate community, headed by the redoubtable Beryl and the Mastersons, carry on their life of pampered luxury in their fortresses on the Peak, in the clubs or at the Captain's Bar in the Mandarin Hotel. While at one level Professor Cobb teaches classical Chinese literature; at another the likes of Jim Connor, an alcoholic Irishman, haunt bars like Swetzo's immortalised later by David Wong. Living on the edge of danger, far from inhibiting anyone, seems to act as a stimulus to even greater frenetic activity.

Only a handful of people move between the European and the Chinese communities: Sister Maria and Father Ignatius are among them. In both cases it is their calling – through the Church – that links them to individuals outside the magic circle. Tom Stewart himself is an unusual *gweilo* because of his relationship with Sister Maria and his entanglement in Chinese society. His long residence in Hong Kong gives him a certain status among the expatriate community whilst his command of Cantonese, an entrée into Chinese society. He takes advantage of both. However, adapted to local culture, he is still a British man living in a British colony with all the privileges that that entails.

# Chapter 13
# A Chinese Wedding: Simon Elegant

Simon Elegant was born in post-war Hong Kong as the city moved into the period of boom depicted in John Lanchester's *Fragrant Harbour,* with large-scale modern buildings taking the place of old, colonial structures and blotting out views of the harbour. New businesses opened up everywhere; former venues took on a new, glossy image. Elegant, of Eurasian background, was educated in Britain and in the United States, where he had a successful career in journalism. He wrote in a wide variety of papers, including the *New York Times* and the *Wall Street Journal* but the lure of Asia brought him back to the Far East. He took charge of *Time* magazine in South East Asia, a job that involved spending time in China. Later he edited the *Far East Economic Review.* His second novel, *The Floating Life*, depicts the life and adventures of Li Po, the eccentric Tang poet much admired by Han Suyin as we have seen. Li Po is reputed to have drowned, having imbibed too much of his much-loved wine while trying to clutch the moon from a boat. A reject from the Confucian exam system, he was an iconoclast and rebel. Elegant's choice of writing the novel about Li Po reveals much about his interest in exploring unconventional characters as well as his considerable knowledge of classical Chinese culture.

In *A Chinese Wedding* Elegant focuses on the differences between Chinese and Western culture in a modern narrative set in the 1990s in Hong Kong. The story is about an intelligent but naive and at times gauche American girl, Amy, and her relationship with a fellow student, Win. He is a Cantonese boy from Hong Kong who has been sent to round off his education in the United States as Elegant himself had done. While appearing to be Westernised in his dress and manners, Win maintains a reserve which makes him seem unapproachable and something of an outsider to American college life. Amy ascribes his reserve to a shyness of character rather than something that stems from a different culture, one in which the individual is caught up in a web of family commitments. While they are both studying in the United States these differences can be put aside. No one there is monitoring their behaviour. However, when Amy agrees to move to Hong Kong as his wife, the situation is entirely changed: Win is once more sucked back into the traditional Chinese family matrix.

The first part of the novel is entirely set in one of the noisy Hong Kong restaurants where the wedding celebrations of the couple are taking place. The waiters and waitresses clatter around the room placing dish after dish on the round tables in front of the seated guests. They seem to be deliberately rude when serving the foreign guests, suggesting an underlying xenophobia. The first thing Amy learns about in their new environment is the overwhelming importance of food. While something of this obsession was evident among the Chinese fraternity at college in the United States:

*the Chinese, at least the six million who live in Hong Kong, are totally absorbed by the getting, the preparation, the presentation and, most important of all, the consumption of food.*[cxix]

A great banquet has been planned for the couple with dozens of families and guests invited by Win's parents. Amy has only just met Win's parents and doesn't know any of the guests. When she tries to engage Win's other relatives in conversation, they are not forthcoming; the expression on one of his sister's face-masks a latent hostility. Even Mei Mei, the most sympathetic, seems entirely boxed in by family tradition, avoiding serious conversation by concentrating on the food being served. In any event most of the conversation is in Cantonese so Amy cannot join in. She feels distinctly uncomfortable in what is supposed to be her own special day.

Amy's parents and brother, who have flown in especially for the occasion are also uncomfortable. Her mother, whom Amy accompanies to the rest rooms, is appalled when she is confronted by an old-fashioned toilet hole in the ground instead of a conventional toilet. She complains bitterly about the noise and filth of the city. She demands to know why Amy has rushed into a marriage with people who are so alien. The thought of half-Chinese grandchildren is not something that appeals to her. Meanwhile at the dining table, Billy, Amy's brother proves to be annoyingly gauche. Without any trace of joking, he asks whether the speed of the couple's marriage was dictated by pregnancy or Win's desire to get a green card so that he can stay in the United States. Amy is not amused. On the other hand, she notices that he has some success in flirting with Win's impassive sisters.

The relationship of Amy and Win to their respective families turns out to be the great divide between them. Win cannot understand why Amy and her siblings have not helped their parents more: her brother Billy more or less ran away from home instead of helping his father run his flagging landscape business. Amy herself has left home. This is not the dutiful behaviour according to Chinese family custom. Amy explains that in America each person looks after him or herself and gets on with his or her life without interference from the family. Win is not taken by this explanation but equally he is he unwilling to say much about his relations with his own family. Amy notices that he never criticises any member of his family and is always respectful to his parents, even when their behaviour does not seem to warrant it. Win is entirely bound by the Confucian system of duty to parents, elders and relatives of the extended family. He tells Amy that the rituals observed between family members are designed to strengthen the bonds between them. They also ultimately hold society together. Under this system any relative turning up from China will be taken in and looked after by the family: there is no other support in the rough and tumble of Hong Kong life.

As the wedding feast continues with course after course, Amy grows more and more uneasy. She knows that her parents, though trying to be outwardly pleasant, are unnerved and deeply upset. She herself begins to panic and wonder whether her impulsive decision to marry Win was a wise one. Endless toasts or *yum sings* are forced on Win by the other guests as he does the rounds of the tables. He becomes steadily more drunk as the banquet drags on. When he reaches the table of the Japanese guests who urge him on, Amy leaps up, snatches the glass from him and gulps down the drink. Everyone is startled; although the guests respond with a cheer, Win is furious. For him it is a great loss of face. His *bonhomie*, his outward politeness and good humour have been shattered by his newlywed's impetuous gesture.

After the wedding banquet which takes up a third of the narrative, the couple move in to live with the Lees in their cramped apartment. This is the beginning of the real test for Amy as Win is out at work all day, often returning late in the evenings, exhausted. She spends a great deal of time confined to their small room, hearing the other members of the family babbling in what sounds like argumentative tones in the corridor. An inconvenient arrangement involves the couple sharing a bathroom with others who can suddenly burst in from an adjoining door. The thin walls of the apartment offer no privacy at all. Some of the sounds Amy can hear are unpleasant throat clearing and spitting noises so that she has to buy ear plugs to blot them out. Even more difficult is the feeling of isolation. Most of the family members are unfriendly and cold, regarding her as an uncouth outsider whom Win should never have married. The sisters are particularly hostile. Even Mei Mei, who at first had seemed the most approachable, becomes cooler while Gah khuin, Win's brother, his wife and children exclude her from the very start. The only person who shows any friendliness is Win's mother who smiles occasionally but says little.

Amy's only escape is to go out. Before long she discovers the brightly-lit stalls of Wanchai market where every kind of fruit and vegetable are sold amid more exotic fare like snakes and tortoises. Pungent smells are only partially allayed by the scent of perfumed jasmine.

*Amy was dazzled by the sheer variety of produce on offer. She counted at least six different kinds of spinach, four kinds of peppers, three kinds of pumpkins, huge white cabbages, all sorts of gnarly root vegetables she did not know. And there was the fruit: papaya, watermelon, apples, oranges and tangerines, odd shaped deep purple fruits, bananas in all sizes.* cxx

The noise of the hawkers shouting out their wares, housewives haggling over prices and coolies carrying huge containers on bamboo poles shouting at people to get out of their way, adds to the bustle. Everyone seems to be in a mad rush whatever the time of day. This was the Hong Kong Amy had come to see: gold-teeth vendors, ladies still in pyjamas and straw hats in the stalls. It was wonderfully exotic and an exciting contrast to suburban America. But these interludes and Amy's secret project of teaching herself Cantonese is not enough to keep her going. Rather against Win's wishes, she lands a job in a news centre. It is run by Dave, a tough, seasoned journalist who doesn't spare his punches. Soon Amy has fallen for him and the two become lovers. The end of her marriage with Win looms in sight.

The narrative of *A Chinese Wedding* is interspersed with flashbacks to Amy's time as a student in the United States telling us more about her background and upbringing. While the to-and-fro is not always easy to follow, the Hong Kong setting itself is convincing. Elegant's portrayal of the Cantonese is well observed: he appreciates their hard-working qualities and loyalty but at the same time casts doubt on the benefit of the family stranglehold. Throughout the telling of the tale, food figures prominently in the Cantonese lifestyle. At the wedding feast Mei Mei, waving her chopsticks at the empty plate on the lazy-Susan, chides Amy for missing the dish of mushrooms which bring good luck.

*I said food is the only important thing at a Chinese wedding. You go away for a few minutes and – whoosh! She waves her hands in the air, smiling. Nothing left but an empty plate. That is how we Cantonese are.*[cxxi]

When the plates are empty the guests will get up and leave; there will be no lingering or lengthy farewells.

And the familiar landmarks of Hong Kong are all there: the Governor's Mansion, the Foreign Correspondents' Club, the skyscraper hotels. Looking out of the windows of an apartment on the slopes of the Peak, Amy sees:

*The great swathe of brilliantly lit buildings stretching away and downwards on either side, the wide black channel of the harbour speckled with the lights of the hundreds of ships at anchor, many of them innocently festive with their fairy lights strung along the rigging, then another vast field of light, glowing white mixed with neon blues and reds and green, Kowloon, the blaze of light thrown up behind it illuminating the underside of the clouds overhead, seeming to stretch on and on, away into China itself.* [cxxii]

But this backcloth is in some ways a cloak over the real city. Elegant reminds us that ninety-seven percent of the population is Chinese. That large mass of people has little or no contact with the glitzy Hong Kong of the colonial elite but they are the real owners of the city.

# Chapter 14
# Kowloon Tong: Paul Theroux

Paul Theroux is a prolific writer, both of travel works and pure fiction. The author of scores of books, numerous articles and occasional pieces, his reputation was clinched by the appearance of the *Great Railway Bazaar* (1975), describing his epic train journey from Britain to Japan. He was brought up in the small town of Medford in Massachusetts where he was schooled, eventually graduating from the University of Massachusetts (Amhurst) with a degree in English in 1963. From there he joined the Peace Corps which had begun to send members to work abroad. He found himself posted in Malawi to teach English.

Theroux's wanderlust thus began in Africa but not without controversy, a characteristic that we shall see repeated in his novel, *Kowloon Tong*, set in Hong Kong just prior to the 1997 handover. In Malawi he became entangled in local politics, helping an Opposition Leader to escape to Uganda. For his part in that episode, he was declared *persona non grata*. At the same time, he was sacked from the Peace Corps. He was able to secure a job at Makere University in Uganda, teaching English, through personal contacts. There he met V.S. Naipaul, a visiting fellow, who became a friend and role model although later, the friendship foundered. He left Uganda under another cloud and began his first connection with the Far East by taking up a post at the National University in Singapore.

Theroux later explained that he had been an angry and disgruntled young man in his African days but held nothing against the continent. His books were banned there, an experience he was to repeat in Singapore when *Saint Jack* (1973) was regarded as highly critical of the regime. He accused Lee Kwan Yew of stifling all dissent, and with it, debate resulting in a sterile public culture. For Theroux Lee Kwan Yew was something of a Hitler-like figure, if one with a heart. Later, his opinion of Tung Chee-hwa, running for the post of chief executive in Hong Kong, was coloured by the latter's stated admiration for Lee Kwan Yew. When he came to set a novel in Hong Kong, his political slant against authority is evident.

When *Kowloon Tong* was reviewed in the *Los Angeles Times*, the headline it ran was 'Mr Grump goes to Hong Kong'. Theroux, like Elegant, tackles the cultural differences between Westerners and the Chinese but his setting is much more political, with the cloud of the handover hanging over. The story begins on the foggy Peak, towering above the city on a cold, damp morning which gives it the feeling of a suburb of London. It is where the Mullard family live: Betty the domineering mother and Bunt, her now middle-aged son. They are served by the somewhat enigmatic Wang, the cook whose mother, Jia, was the family *amah* for a long period. While Betty Mullard is contemptuous of the Chinese, 'Chinky-Chonks' as she disparagingly calls them, Bunt, brought up in Hong Kong, has slightly more empathy with the locals. Like all colonial children he has been influenced by the servants who looked after him as a child. However, like his mother, he cannot abide their food. Mother and son make an odd couple, getting along by ignoring traits in each other's character which irritate them.

The family own a factory, *Imperial Stitching* which does well in the colonial environment of loose regulation and low taxes. They employ 200 staff and among other items, produce badges for clubs and schools, sometimes embroidered with royal insignia. The business had been a venture of Bunt's father and a Mr. Chuck, a refugee from mainland China. Like so many arrivals from the mainland, he fears an invasion and the end of his business in Hong Kong. When the factory was being sited, Mr Chuck is superstitious enough to call in a geomancer to check that the *feng shui* was favourable. Tucked under the shadow of the nine dragon hills, Kowloon Tong (nine dragon's pond) was chosen as the right location.

Mr Chuck provided much of the capital for the business but having a British partner was greatly advantageous. Both men were keen entrepreneurs, plunging into the frenzy of the rebuilding of post-war Hong Kong. When Mr Mullard died, Mr Chuck took over the entire running of the business teaching Bunt the tricks of the trade he had learned over a lifetime. He also acted as surrogate family to the Mullards and became 'uncle' to Bunt in the traditional Chinese way. When he in turn passed away, he left his entire share of the business to Bunt who now had to run it on his own, without his 'uncle's' astute business sense to fall back on.

Bunt is a queer fish. Trapped between his mother's tight regime at home and the routine tedium of the factory, his only outlet is to visit local bars where he can find female companions. His haunts are the Pussy Cat Club and the Happy Bar which he is amused to discover were frequented by his father and by Mr Chuck in their time. Taking his lunchtime sandwiches, with the edges carefully trimmed by Wang, the cook, he enjoys a San Miguel beer before retiring to a cubicle with one of the girls. Bunt's whole life has been in Hong Kong, so that he knows little about England where he has only been on visits. Yet he also seems sheltered from much of Hong Kong life outside the narrow circuit of his home, *Imperial Stitching* and the molly houses. He completely blots out listening to any news about the handover scheduled for the following year, resolutely refusing to consider any alternative to carrying on with the factory. He has no intention of leaving and does not believe that a change of flag will make much difference to his life style. His mother, on the other hand, follows the news closely and predicts the worst once 'Chinky Chonk' take over. She is actively looking for an escape route, preferably one that leads them back to England with a nest egg to live on.

Betty Mullard is an extremely unsympathetic character. From her fairly humble social background in Balham, she has turned into the stereotype Hong Kong ex-patriate who has no interest in Chinese culture. She never eats Chinese food or allows it to be cooked at home. She harbours racist sentiments about the Chinese whom she regards as an inferior race. Not only was it a myth that they were enigmatic and mysterious but, in her view, they were unsubtle and unambiguous, bordering on the crass. Their frugality ended when it came to gambling, either on horses at Happy Valley or on the card tables of the casinos in Macau. Betty is also an unrelenting snob, sneering at people whose accent is, like her own, not pukka. Her life is passed in isolation on the Peak or among equally-minded bigots for afternoon tea in the Hong Kong Club or the lobby of one of the leading hotels.

It is perhaps surprising that Betty Mullard is the one who reacts most favourably to the appearance of the sinister Mr Hung in their lives. Hung arrives unannounced at *Imperial Stitching* with an offer to buy the factory. Bunt finds him different from any local Chinese person and is highly suspicious of him:

*He had looked Bunt in the eye, as Singaporeans did, but his English was far better than that of any Hong Kong or Singapore Chinese, and from its precision and over correctness Bunt concluded that the man was from China. He had gone to a good school. He had been force-fed the English language in the brainwashing way of Chinese education, and had learned it for a purpose, which was to con and cheat English-speaking people.*[cxxiii]

Hung's offer comes with a threat that after the handover, the Mullards will be forced to accept a much lower price for the factory than the millions he has put on the table. Indeed, he assures them that it would most likely be seized by the new regime without any compensation, leaving them penniless. He senses a difference of approach between the mother and son. So as to advance his cause, unknown to Bunt, Hung ingratiates himself with Betty Mullard enticing her with the thought of the luxurious lifestyle she will be able to lead once the sale has been completed. He also finds out about Bunt's private visits to the clubs and his various liaisons with employees at the factory.

At first Bunt resists his offer out of hand but Hung persists. In an unusual gesture in Hong Kong, where most encounters take place outside the home in hotels or restaurants, he invites Bunt to his apartment, located a stone's throw away from *Imperial Stitching*. Bunt cannot resist seeing Hung's den: the place is shoddy and impersonal as he expects, with touches of the kitsch. Hung presents him with a cheap bunch of gifts, equally tasteless.

Eventually under pressure from his mother and advice from Monty, an opportunist lawyer who appears as Hung's adviser, Bunt gives in after meeting Hung at the Pussy Cat and being told that his mother is one hundred percent behind the deal. But no sooner has he agreed the sale when he regrets it; Betty's joy at 'a million quid' makes him feel even more dejected. Betty herself is ecstatic, she seizes the opportunity to spend part of their advance on gambling on the horses at Happy Valley and even plans a trip to Macau to visit the casinos. She has always despised the Chinese workforce at the factory and gloats on the idea that they will be punished for their ingratitude. She also considers that leaving Hong Kong on the terms under offer is a victory: Hung has overestimated the value of the factory.

During the time when the deal was being worked out, Hung made various overtures to Bunt, gloating at his success in forcing the sale. One invitation is to dinner at the Golden Dragon Restaurant even though he knows that the Englishman would not touch the Chinese food put before him. To show his power and to add to Bunt's humiliation, Hung brings two employees of *Imperial Stitching* with him, Mei-Ping whom Bunt fancies and Ah Fu, her flatmate. Bunt is disconcerted by the appearance of the two ladies as Hung's guests suggesting a conspiracy involving them all. At the table Hung places Mei-ping near to Bunt, keeping Ah Fu close to himself. The ladies are subdued and seem frightened by Hung's overbearing manner. His appearance is demonic, his lips gleaming with the brandy he has been drinking.

*Bunt remembered the look of greed, of heedless hunger, he had seen on Hung's face in the lounge of the Regent. It was the face of the desperate peasant who had been wrenched from his village and plunked down in luxury. Hung had not known that Bunt was staring at him: that was Hung's real face.*[cxxiv]

In a sinister sequel to the outing, Ah Fu completely vanishes, leaving Mei-ping utterly distraught. She begs Bunt to find out what has happened to her companion. After putting things off for some days, Bunt decides to pay an unannounced visit to Hung's apartment. Hung will not let him in at once and since Bunt insists, tells him to return later. When Bunt is finally allowed to enter the flat, he notices missing items such as the carpet which suggest that they have been removed because of damage and possibly blood stains. He begins to suspect something sadistic has taken place in the flat and that Hung has murdered Ah Fu. When he confronts Hung:

*Hung's mask was his expression of facing a high wind, cheeks sucked in, eyes narrowed to slits, giving nothing away. It was the making of poker faces in which the Chinese were expert.*[cxxv]

At the same time Bunt realises that his feeling for Mei-ping amounts to more than carnal desire. He has always been attracted to her boyish figure and her demure manner but now an emotional element is introduced. He feels the need to protect her from the threatening atmosphere of Hung's takeover, especially as she seems so frightened and vulnerable. The feeling is a powerful one and leads to some fantasy on Bunt's part.

*He imagined arriving in London with Mei-ping: having her on his arm, buying her meals, showing her the sights. So engrossed was he that he could not see himself in London without her.*[cxxvi]

He has fallen in love. Mei-ping is depressed and terrified at the thought that she may be the next victim on Hung's list. In an impulsive moment Bunt decides to elope with her to Macau. On the hydrofoil the nightmarish details of her escape from China come flooding back and she longs to escape.

Macau is reassuringly sleepy and quiet compared to Hong Kong. There seems something sad in its atmosphere but the mood suits the couple well. They check into the Bela Vista Hotel, an old colonial relic where the receptionist is wearing a badge embroidered with the Imperial Stitching logo. The hotel has a pleasant, old world feeling where the couple feel safe. They retire to a comfortable room, with high ceilings and a view down to the *praia* or seafront. Lying on the bed in their room, both stretch out without touching one another while Mei-ping tells Bunt the story of her escape from China on a fishing boat down the stormy Pearl River. It is a grisly tale: thinking he was her saviour, Mei-ping was raped by the fisherman who acted as her rescuer. Fleeing with her was a pregnant Ah Fu so that a strong bond between them was formed by the time they landed in Lantau. In Hong Kong they share a tiny apartment and both get jobs at *Imperial Stitching*.

The lovers' escape to Macau does not end well. Bunt's impulse to have a flutter on the gambling tables of the casino of the Lisboa hotel has an unforeseen consequence that wrecks their plan to stay overnight in the spacious, comfortable room at the Bela Vista: Betty Mullard turns out to have also made the journey to Macau and is in the same casino, gambling at the tables. She spots the couple and, as usual, takes control. Saying that she has finished for the day, she orders Bunt and Mei-ping to leave with her on the next hydro-foil back to Hong Kong. The lovers meekly obey.

The story ends on a desperately sad note. Monty, Hung's agent in the business settlement, suddenly informs the Mullards that they must leave Hong Kong at once in order to comply with the settlement over the sale of the factory. Tickets have been booked on a flight to London; a car is arranged to take them to the airport. On the way there, Bunt manages to force them to stop at *Imperial Stitching* and rushes into the factory searching for Mei-ping. But there is no sign of her; the factory is deserted. Nor does she answer her phone when he repeatedly tries to call her. The Mullards are hurried onto the plane; when it takes off there is a sinister suggestion that Betty has been in league with Hung to get rid of Mei-ping. While Bunt is thoroughly depressed, she seems concerned only with getting a drink served on board. Her domination of Bunt is again complete.

In Kowloon Tong the bulldozers soon move in and demolish the factory, watched by a crowd including some of *Imperial Stitching* staff. They look on as everything comes crashing down, hurrying away once the *ch'i* or spirit has been released. It is a sad scene:

*Then the site was empty, just broken stones with the junked and rubbly look of reclaimed land, and sitting on it was the long-necked crane, like a green dragon with a toy in its mouth.*[cxxvii]

While certain parts of the novel are set in regular Hong Kong places – the Mullards live on the Peak, they frequent the Hong Kong Club and Cricket Club in Central – the local area where the factory is located, Kowloon Tong, is a district not so well known to the *gweilo* community. It is a less sophisticated part of Kowloon where the bars are inexpensive and the girls in them more friendly than their counterparts in Wanchai or Tsim Sha Tsui. Setting the novel in this less known area gives it a certain, local flavour different from many of the other stories accounts of Hong Kong during this period. One reviewer does, however question whether the streets there were really 'crawling with Chinese and Filipino call girls'. [cxxviii]

Theroux's portrait of the characters, both British, Chinese and even American, is thoroughly negative. The British are snobbish upstarts who have come from quite ordinary backgrounds at home to lord it over the downtrodden locals. Exemplified by Betty Mullard, they move in confined circles and have no interest in the society outside of their colonial bubble. It is an insular community which seems entirely remote from the reality of what is about to happen. Bunt exemplifies this attitude by refusing to listen to the news as the handover looms. The colonial ladies assemble to gossip and past their time in trivial pursuits. Meanwhile the men, unless downing their San Miguel beer in the acceptable venues like the Hong Kong Club, spend their free time in seedy bars picking up local girls.

Although the ex-patriates moan about their lives in Hong Kong, they have no real desire to return to the United Kingdom, having got used to their pampered, insular existence. Other foreigners, like the American Hoyt Maybry, are highly unsavoury, taking out foreign nationalities to continue in their dubious business practices while also enjoying all the benefits of the high life. Theroux uses the character of Hoyt to express his dislike of the British, colonial regime.

'Hong Kong is an accident of history' Hoyt declares 'that is about to be rectified'. [cxxix] It had never been a democratic society; the old school tie was all that mattered among its elite. Foreigners were only grudgingly admitted into the magic circle. Even so for an astute businessman like Hoyt, money was to be made as it always was in times of change. One just had to adapt to the new circumstances, in any case easier when one was a critic of the old.

The Cantonese do not come over in a better light. Their language makes them sound as if they are snarling; filthy habits like spitting in the streets are commonplace and no one can be trusted in business deals. Frugal on the one hand, they are reckless gamblers on the other. The outwardly calm demeanour can suddenly turn into a violent outburst of foul language and aggressive behaviour. Even servants who have worked for decades with British employers, like Wang, seem remote and living in a different world. The wealthy among them continue to lead a luxurious life style far removed from the masses who serve them and whose welfare seems of no concern to them. Like the expatriates, they are pampered by retinues of servants and hangers-on. When they are involved in business, like the partners of the untrustworthy Monty, they take out foreign nationality, obtaining passports from Canada to the Cayman Islands as insurance in case they too have to make a sudden exit.

In an interview at the time of the handover, Theroux claimed that he wrote the novel in order to capture 'the soul of the people'.[cxxx] V.S. Naipaul had told him that a book needs a reason for being written: as the handover looms there is every reason to write one. However, on another, later occasion, Theroux says he cannot understand Hong Kong:

*I feel lost in Hong Kong. I don't know how you would write about it; it is impenetrable. There's so much of it… I don't mean writing about the restaurants and hotels; I mean about the city itself. You'd have to live there to do that.*[cxxxi]

Nevertheless, despite these reservations, he claims that in *Kowloon Tong* he has captured all the sounds, smells and feelings that he felt about Hong Kong. That can only be done by describing the names of streets and people's emotions. Moreover, he was compelled to write it because the story of the place before the handover had to be told in personal terms. He links one enduring characteristic of Hong Kong – the obsessive pursuit of money, remarked upon by writers from Austin Coates to Xu Xi, – to a lack of freedom to do anything else. It is the only available occupation, spurred on by the feeling that the good times might suddenly end. Those who are able to look for escape routes, in some cases setting up homes abroad, to be ready to flee should the worst happen.

One characteristic of the situation in 1996 was an echo of 1949 as Austin Coates had said, namely that Hong Kong remained entirely insular, paying little attention to what was happening in China. It existed in a bubble of its own, even though its lifestyle was once again threatened with being entirely changed. Most Hong Kongers had never set foot on the mainland:

*China is such an exotic, strange, menacing place to people living in Hong Kong that they just can't imagine it.*[cxxxii]

Theroux claims that the racism inherent in the narrative is just a representation of the colony as it was in its last phase. The division between the ethnic groups is as strong as ever with the British expatriates and wealthy Chinese hardly mingling socially. He accepts that the characters in his story are, to some extent, caricatures of both the British and the Chinese. Yet the colonial way of life, with its social divisions, has become part of the local culture for better or worse. It makes Hong Kong quite different from any other city in China. In setting out to satirise the departing British, he says that the characters he presents are bound to be racist. But his satire includes showing up the dark side of Beijing's methods of control (principally through the character of Hung) and of unscrupulous American business men (in the character of Hoyt). Hung is not only an opportunist in the sense of wanting to make a killing by buying the factory but he is a power grabber who relishes the tremendous influence that he exerts over other characters in the book. The overall picture is a bleak one and has led one Hong Kong reviewer asking why Theroux felt the need to 'do such a disservice to the place that is my home'. [cxxxiii]

In an important respect, Theroux misunderstands what would be involved in the hand-over. He seems to envisage China taking over the running of Hong Kong from day one with the People's Liberation Army prominently marching in the streets. The regime, overnight, will become entirely inflexible and the city will be cut off from its foreign roots. Everything will change at once; history will be rewritten and only foreigners useful to the regime will be allowed to remain. For dramatic purposes in the novel, he sticks to that scenario: Hung represents all that is clandestine and secretive about China but he will be in the vanguard when the take-over occurs. So Hung is able to threaten the Mullards into getting his way by painting a grim picture of what their position and that of all *gweilos* will be after the hand-over.

In fact, there was little immediate change in Hong Kong in 1997 as Janice Lee noticed on her return in 2005. Indeed, the development of democracy which itself was fairly recent, continued with contested local elections and elections to the Legislative Council. Unsurprisingly there were pro-Beijing supporters among the candidates but also there were plenty of pro-democracy supporters who gained a significant number of seats in the Council. Hong Kong had entered yet another phase of its development. From being ruled by a colonial regime with a light touch, protecting the rule of law, it had become a self-governing community with its own leaders, even if some pledged loyalty to China rather than Hong Kong. But this new stage took place under the umbrella of the 'one country, two systems' principle agreed between China and Britain.

The idea of Hong Kong becoming an independent republic like Singapore, which Theroux supports, is entirely at odds with this political settlement and impossible for the Chinese to accept. In their view the 'Fragrant Harbour' had been torn away from China after one of the greatest humiliations she had suffered in the Opium War. One day, but not until it suits China, there will be a complete take over. Then the loss of face of the past would be wiped out. But that would not be in 1997.

# Chapter 15
# Hammer and Tong: David T K Wong

David T K Wong has led a nomadic life including periods in China, Singapore, Australia, the United States, the United Kingdom, and of course, in the place of his birth, Hong Kong. When he was an infant of three years old, the family moved to Canton but on the breakup of his parents' marriage he was sent to Singapore to live with his grandparents. After his schooling there he emigrated, as a refugee, to Australia at the outbreak of war. His penniless status at that time inspired sympathy with the underdog, a theme that emerges frequently in his short stories. He later gained a degree at Stanford University in the United States and completed post-graduate studies in the Hague. His career has been as varied as the places he has lived in: journalist, public official, businessman and educator, his abiding passion and motivation has been to write.

In an interview he gave in the 1990s he said that his dream had been not only to record his own experience but also the ups and downs of the human condition in all its rawness. Sharing his observations and feeling with his reader was also linked to his desire to explain aspects of social history in highly personal terms. That is a legacy that he wants to leave to posterity but he is motivated to encourage others to write fiction as well. Towards that end he has endowed a trust to support creative writing, enabling new generations of writers be future torchbearers. He also sees his impulse to write as a means of liberation, something that might serve to ease the conflict and muddle of different cultures vying with one another for supremacy. While trying to craft words beautifully, the writer must also contribute to the betterment of understanding. Like anyone else, he wants to avoid penury but at the same time he has a pedagogic role to play.

The medium through which Wong has most successfully achieved his objective is that of the short story. It began with success in an essay competition when his talent was spotted by a perceptive publisher. Thereafter a number of his stories appeared in magazines and journals and were broadcast on radio networks around the world. A complete collection appeared in 1996. The characters of his stories come from every walk of life: successful businessmen, bureaucrats, labourers, bartenders and call girls, many of whom are refugees from mainland China who have come to Hong Kong believing its streets to be paved with gold. There is often a note of irony in his portraits of successful individuals who have entered the upper echelons of society.

K. B. Woo, known just as 'K. B.' is one such character:

*As the most famous tycoon in a city replete with taipans and captains of industry, he is the darling of the cocktail cult. His name figures in the invitation lists of virtually everybody pretending to the upper crust. It is not unusual, therefore, for him to attend three or four cocktail parties in a single day.*[cxxxiv]

However, K.B. does so grudgingly; he is not impressed by the glitter of the pretentious cocktail-party circuit and does the rounds solely for the purpose of networking and staving off gossip from the newsmongers who would comment on his absence. He arrives at one party in a particularly nostalgic mood because it marks the agreed end of his affair with an attractive and vivacious pick up, Lulu. To his shock and surprise, it turns out that Lulu has in fact hitched herself up to a fellow businessman of K.B.'s own age. As the pair come forward to greet him, K.B. cannot show any sign of recognition which would acknowledge his own liaison with Lulu, let alone display any emotional reaction. She too must play her part pretending not to know him. Like many of Wong's characters, K. B. can only look back at his life with regret, cursing himself for not having teamed up with Lulu, prevented by inappropriate British law from having her as a concubine, a perfectly sensible arrangement.

The theme of lost opportunity and the nostalgia that comes with it, especially in later life, appears again in 'Lost River'. This time there is a gender switch: Jasmine is back in London, on a rare visit, remembering her early student days and involvement with Arnold in the dreary boarding house where they both lodged. Arnold is an attractive, sandy-haired writer fired with an idealism that makes him indifferent to joining the rat race and making money. When the couple move to their own flat, Jasmine's father appears from Hong Kong to rescue his daughter from marriage to an impoverished writer. The idea that their union might lead to his having grandchildren with blue eyes and no notion of Chinese culture fills him with horror. Years later, on her lonely return to London, Jasmine tries to track down Arnold. She discovers that he has become Sales Director of a firm but does not follow it up by meeting him.

In another story 'Julia' the hero is Peng who:

*Was everything Chinese parents could possibly expect of their son at the age of nineteen. He was diligent, well-mannered, filial and outstanding both academically and in sports. He cut a splendid figure too, being clear-skinned and straight-limbed, with a carriage that was smart and erect.*[cxxxv]

While studying in England Peng mixes with a bohemian crowd which includes the buxom and promiscuous Julia. Invited to stay the weekend at her country retreat, he is enticed into her boudoir but holds back, refusing to be led astray despite his carnal desire for her. Peng knows that his parents will disapprove of Julia and abhor any relationship he might have with her. His Chinese upbringing had not prepared him for a Julia. But years later, established in Hong Kong as Chief Economist of a leading bank, he cannot help reflecting on his own agonising ambivalence which may have lost him a life of adventure and happiness.

A number of Wong's stories deal with the harsh lives of the underprivileged, particularly refugees from mainland China lured by the prospect of a better life. In 'Red, Amber, Green' Old Mak is a rickshaw-puller whose life has become more and more difficult on the motor-crowded roads of Hong Kong. In China one disaster after another, drought followed by typhoons, destroyed his family's farm and reduced him and his mother to being manual workers in fields they no longer owned. When his mother died, Old Mak made the decision to flee to Hong Kong 'to earn his passage to the Golden Mountain'.[cxxxvi] Eking out a living during the Japanese occupation, worse followed after the war. To ease a throbbing pain in his chest, he took to smoking opium but when the pipes he used are found in this hovel he is arrested and charged with possession of illegal goods. The trial process baffles him since his only intention is to tell the truth. He is found guilty and sentenced to imprisonment but, ironically, this proves a god-sent. After several months in jail, he will be deported to his native Kwantung. He is delighted:

*Life might be hard on the land but at least a man was free to live according to his own rhythm. If he walked about his village at night to admire the brilliance of the moon or to enjoy the song of the cicadas, he would not be accused of committing a crime.*[cxxxvii]

Another illegal immigrant is Yun in 'The Revolt of the Grasses' who is working on a building site in Hong Kong's construction boom. Like his fellow workers, his life is controlled by a shadowy organisation which smuggles workers in from the mainland. They are paid paltry wages from which the obese Fatty Fong, the controller, takes ten percent. He disappears the moment there is any trouble and the workers are left to fend for themselves. When there is a police raid on the building where they immigrants are working and everyone is ordered down from the bamboo scaffoldings, Yun refuses to move edging further away from the ledge and waiting for the dawn.

Given the post-war boom in Hong Kong one of Wong's stories was bound to be set in the squatters' camps. 'Blood Debt' involves a police officer, Hung who himself began life in Squatters Hill, a refugee with his father from Mao's Cultural Revolution. His family owe a debt to the Ma family who saved them from intimidation by a local gang. According to Chinese custom, the debt has to be repaid. This turns to be a dangerous legacy as in the meantime young Ma has become involved in various illegal activities. He taunts Hung with being nothing more than a colonial lackey and eventually draws Hung into his web of corruption. When Hung realises that he has entirely implicated himself in a tangle from which there is no escape, he commits suicide with his police revolver, young Ma rushing towards him in horror.

Wong is equally concerned with exposing the double standards and hypocrisy of the mixed Chinese and expatriate world which makes up the better off section of Hong Kong society. A character in the middle of this nexus is Swetzo who runs a bar in Soho. He is something of an enigmatic character: well-travelled and an impressive master of a number of languages. The only qualification for membership of the bar is to be a good imbiber. His array of customers includes bored expatriates, businessmen, artists and writers all given to heavy drinking and who, in their way, are the flotsam and jetsam of local society. Swetzo's bar does not close until the last customer leaves, usually highly inebriated. One of these 'bar-flys' in Yuen who regrets not returning from the United States where he was studying in time to take up his life with Ching Ching, his girlfriend in Hong Kong. When he does finally return it is too late: she has been forced into a life of prostitution to keep herself and her mother afloat.

Swetzo re-appears in 'A Dusty Road'. He is a friend of the Chief Secretary, a onetime frequenter of his bar who now lies dying of cancer in a private ward in Queen Mary Hospital. The grand administrator has his regrets at not taking up with Jenny, a Eurasian pick up girl whose appearance makes him unable to tell whether she is Chinese or not. Her nose was rather straighter than was normal for a Chinese. Lying on his hospital bed, he cannot help thinking of her without a dull, unforgiving ache. Unexpectedly, Jenny makes an appearance in the hospital and to ensure her financial future, the Chief Secretary arranges to marry her on his deathbed. He derives macabre pleasure in thinking of his colleagues gathering at his funeral with Jenny present.

Other stories deal with the breakdown of traditional Chinese family values in modern Hong Kong. Ah Soong, always referred to as 'Old Soong', is a highly cultivated scholar in the old Chinese style who also specialises in the arcane art of making seals. His English friend, Middleton, becomes fascinated by seals and apprentices himself to 'Old Soong'. Although 'Old Soong' is a hard taskmaster, the two become firm friends: Middleton is godfather to Sing-Yee, 'Old Soong's' son. Sing-Yee rebelling at his father's dominance, refuses to be drawn into his world, instead opting for a career in finance at which he proves very successful. Father and son are totally estranged from one another; for 'Old Soong' it is a dire warning that the lure of modern life with its technology will destroy a culture that has withstood invasion from Huns, Mongols and Manchus.

In 'Hammer and Tong' the scene shifts to the internal works of government, something Wong is closely familiar with from his time as a civil servant himself. Mumford, an administrator who is about to retire, finds a note that reminds him of an unfortunate episode in his career involving a cover-up. He and his boss at the time failed in the task of grooming Tong, a redoubtable young Chinese assistant, to take up high office as the handover approaches. Instead of proving reliable as the two officials have pledged, Tong disappears while on a course in England. The Secretariat stands to be ridiculed for what has turned out to be a fiasco involving the waste of public funds. The file containing all the details of this unfortunate episode has to be lost.

Wong's short stories move between the colonial, upper wrapping of Hong Kong and the Chinese culture that underlies it. His exposure of this contrast is done through descriptions of individuals rather than in the familiar settings of

Hong Kong – the hotels, clubs and crowded streets – Keung, for example in 'Voices in the Heart', has ageless features 'remarkable even for a Chinese, for he was not far from sixty'.[cxxxviii] Through his many characters, Wong sketches the unexpected twists and disappointments of life. Yet his characters do not seem to baulk at the injustices of the world they find themselves in. There is a stoical acceptance of fate.

Wong's characterisation of Hong Kong people is taken to greater lengths and depths in his novel, *The Evergreen Tea House* (2003). The episodic format he uses reminds us that he is a short story writer at heart, used to succinct presentation in an Oriental style. The narrative is made up of a sequence of short chapters in different settings, spanning a long period from 1952 to 1985. At times this is a complicated path for the reader to follow. Not all the story is set in Hong Kong; there are intervals in China itself and elsewhere but in one way or another all the characters are connected to Hong Kong and the events unfolding in the colony.

The principal character in the narrative is Chu Wing-seng, the son of a highly successful Hong Kong business magnate, Chu Tung. The story begins on an outing that young Chu Wing-seng makes with his friend, Little Ho, as a boy scout to capture snakes, prized as ingredients in Cantonese cuisine. The boys pass through typical Hong Kong scenes on their way to remoter parts of the colony. In the narrow, cobblestone streets there are shops where everything from wooden scrubbing boards to writing brushes are sold:

*There were bakeries, noodle shops and small eateries, as well as the odd letter-writer, cobbler, barber, herbalist and seller of tropical fish.[cxxxix]*

Chu Wing-seng is actually afraid of snakes but Little Ho, older than him, guides him carefully. Little Ho is a compassionate, idealistic boy who believes in helping everyone, something which Wong suggests is rare in Hong Kong where each man is for himself. He protects Chu Wing-sen but in such a way that his friend does not lose face.

Chu Tung has built up a great empire based on the Gold Star Corporation of which he is the chairman and main shareholder. Despite his great financial success, Chu Tung is riddled with self-doubt. His business enterprise began during the Japanese occupation of Hong Kong when food supplies had dwindled to an alarmingly low level. With a group of collaborators, calling themselves the

'Evergreens' he directed a smuggling operation bringing in supplies from China which were snapped up by locals with disposable assets. The demand for these goods soared and the Evergreens became rich. After the war they invested their gains in various businesses as Hong Kong revived and its black-market economy boomed.

Although Chu Tung considered that he had always played by the rules, exploiting what was a ruthless capitalist environment made him feel guilty, knowing that his success has meant the ruin of many small businesses. It was a far cry from the Confucian ideal of self-sacrifice that a leader was supposed to show. Moreover, Chu Tung was a man of some culture. He accumulated a valuable collection of Chinese art and *objets* as well as a library which focussed on rare books which extolled the virtues of learning and scholarship. His collection was housed in the grand mansion that he had built on the prestigious upper slopes of the Peak. An inner sanctum with his most valuable pieces was kept under lock and key.

Chu Tung tries to induce a respect for ancient Chinese culture in his son but with little success. The Tang poets, the analects of Confucius and the Ming ceramics make no impression on Chu Wing-seng whose motivation is to emulate and even exceed his father's business success. Nor is he attracted to the Buddhist practices of his mother, Serenity, mainly carried out in the quiet of the Meditation Room which has been specially set up for her in the mansion. His parents seem to conspire to turn him away from business towards becoming a man of learning and refinement, something Chu Wing-seng simply cannot understand. Instead, he sets his sights on studying financial and business management in one of the leading American institutions although his father is sceptical of the benefits of such an education even for someone who wants to enter the rough and tumble of real business.

While this scene is being set in Hong Kong, Wong portrays another in a remote village in China called 'Thirsty Hills' due to the lack of local rainfall. In this case the young protagonist is Cheng Ching whose parents are peasant farmers eking out a living from the barren land where they live. His father, Cheng Yen, is severely handicapped having lost both his legs when fighting for the Communist cause in the famous battle of the Luting Bridge, a milestone in Mao's ascendency. He hopes that his son will take over the back-breaking work on the farm. However, Cheng Ching, like Chu Wing-seng, wants to emulate his father, in this case to take up the cause by joining up as a soldier for action in Korea where war is raging.

Cheng Yen has to pretend that he is not perturbed by his son's decision. As a young man, he himself had run away to join the Red Army without any leave-taking of his father whom he never saw again. Not wanting that experience to be repeated and at the same time to save face by not appearing upset, he prepares a proper farewell, giving his son some medicines including one that stems the flow of blood in injuries. Cheng Ching's experience on the battlefields of Korea is harrowing. He witnesses the injury and death of close companions. One incident above all others totally destroys his belief in war. He confronts a wounded American soldier – a young fellow like himself but with fair hair and blue eyes – whom he wants to help. The American does not understand what he says and fires at him. Cheng Ching's return fire kills the man. But he is haunted by the experience which he relates to the nurse Ying the next day adding another woeful experience on his own side:

*Yesterday I looked into the eyes of a stranger and blew his brains out. I watched him spill onto the ground. It was revolting. Today I knelt beside a man whom I had played chess with and watched his life ebb away. It was every bit as bad. Such things are too hard for me. I can't stand them anymore. I would rather die.*[cxl]

Despite his repulsion at all the violence he has seen, Ching is destined for great things within the folds of the Party. He and Ying are chosen to visit Peking. There he is introduced to Mao who praises the sacrifice of his father at Luting Bridge and enlists Cheng Ching to support the Party. At the same time, eying the beautiful Ying, Mao sucks her into the internal cadre of comrades that protect him day and night. Ching is over-awed by Mao but deeply resentful of the abduction of Ying with whom he has become infatuated. He is sent to Hong Kong to mastermind intelligence on behalf of the motherland.

Meanwhile in Hong Kong the younger Chu has adopted Xavier as his first name. He believes that by changing his name he is projecting a new image for the Gold Star Corporation following his father's death in unexplained circumstances, something which the press link to rumours about his secret, sex life. Sorting through company papers, Xavier notices a larger than expected bill from the Evergreen Tea House, the regular rendezvous of the Evergreens in a back street in Western. He decides to pay a visit to the tea house to find out what has led to the inflated account. The establishment is a throwback to another time:

*It was set in a row of two-storied tenements, each with its own outdated charm. The marble cloud-patterned table top, set in a blackwood frame, had long gone out of fashion. Four identical booths, separated by high latticed wooden panels, flanked both sides of the room. The space in between was occupied by three round tables, each with six matching stools. A large brass spittoon stood next to each booth. Lazy ceiling fans made a pretence at ventilation.[cxli]*

Xavier is greeted by Uncle Yue, his father's closest companion who offers him Dragon's Well Tea when he has asked for a coke. Uncle Yue takes his time pouring the tea, pointing to pictures on the wall which portray a Sung dynasty calligrapher and his companion, a well-educated courtesan who can discuss art and literature with the master. He expounds on the virtues of different varieties of tea, each aiding recovery from different ailments from bad digestion to poor blood circulation. None of this conversation interests Xavier who is now obsessed with business and making a fortune even greater than his father's. Eventually Uncle Hue comes to the point, telling Xavier that the additional expense is because the Evergreens hire the first floor of the tea house exclusively for their own use. However, the bonus for doing so is in the arrangements laid on for their meals and eating, the usual Cantonese preoccupation. Uncle Hue explains:

*But this place is special. It serves the usual dim sum, but for special customers it lays on the best and freshest foods from the markets each day. It means pot luck, of course. We'll just have to enjoy our tea and wait to see what we get.[cxlii]*

Xavier is not admitted to the magic circle of the Evergreens straight away; Uncle Yue recommends that he comes regularly to the tea house and gradually gets to know the fraternity. In due course he will be admitted as a full member.

Meanwhile Xavier has married Lucille. She was a fellow student in the United States who was brought up in the Chinatown of San Francisco where her parents ran a modest fruit shop. Caught between two worlds, on the one hand saluting the Stars and Stripes at school each morning and on the other, speaking the Toi Shan dialect at home, Lucille is unsure of her identity. Is she Chinese or

American? For her conservative parents Xavier is a suitable husband: from a rich family, absolutely Chinese he will provide them with the much-awaited grandson that they so much hanker after. While the couple are students together, Xavier seems relaxed but once back in Hong Kong, he joins the hectic rat race to making more and more money. He only returns late at night each day with little time to attend to their sickly son, Ah Yuen or the sexual longings of his wife.

Lucille, disillusioned by life at home but not daring to upset both families begins a clandestine affair with Sebastian Baxingdale, a British journalist known for his forthright reporting. Baxingdale's first Hong Kong experience was as a British soldier serving on the border post with China. He witnessed the capturing and return to China of refugees desperate to get into the colony with a sense of disgust and guilt. He joins Soames, an alcoholic middle grade civil servant in exposing the corruption of the colonial regime and its continuous prevarications over policy with China. The narrative ends on a tragic note for both parties. Xavier disappears in Taiwan where he is murdered by the brothers of Fei Fei, a dancing girl with whom he had been infatuated and whose trail he had been following. In the meantime, Baxingdale has departed for England without Lucille.

The political background is ever present in Wong's story. As the handover of the colony to China looms, there is an even more frenetic attempt to make money, shared by both the pro and anti-British upper crust of Chinese entrepreneurs. Meanwhile the Communist infiltration of Hong Kong continues under the direction of Cheng Ching in an elaborate underground network. Local disturbances gain momentum with daily riots. The British elite seem unaware of this, continuing to lead their privileged lives as if nothing was happening as we have seen in Christopher New's the Chinese Box.

Baxingdale does not feel part of the colonial clique, finding his fellow countrymen smug and over-confident. He observes that:

*The expatriate top brass seemed to live in splendid isolation, oblivious of the fact that ninety-eight percent of the population was Chinese. He [Baxingdale] however, felt troubled by that isolation. He wished he knew Chinese, so that he could discover what made them tick and how they thought the British rule impacted upon their lives.*[cxliii]

He is an unusual example of a displaced *gweilo* or foreigner rather than being a displaced Eurasian or Chinese who has been educated abroad. But his friend Knight warns him:

*Don't romanticize. Hong Kong's just a mongrel city, a new Babylon, more freebooting by the day. It's entirely market driven. The realisation of everything that Adam Smith wrote about, except the emphasis on education. Between now and 1997 there're fortunes to be made for those with enough gumption to find their own niches.* [cxliv]

Wong is not disinclined to take a swipe at the British lack of care about their local subjects with 'a wrong skin pigmentation'.[cxlv] With its myriad of distinct and separate societies, all coexisting without merging, lubricated by money, Wong's Hong Kong of 1985 has not essentially changed since the 1950s colony of Austin Coates and Martin Booth.

# Chapter 16
# Atlas of An Imaginary City:
# Dung Kai-Cheung

Dung Kai-cheung is a born and bred Hong Konger. His family had moved there from China before he was born in 1967. He grew up in the boom period when Kowloon was becoming densely populated by the flow of refugees, as we have seen in *Diamond Hill*. Like Feng Chi-shun he also went to La Salle college, proving again it has been a breeding ground for distinguished alumni whatever its reputation for producing the tough boys Feng Chi-shun described. From school Dung went to Hong Kong University to study comparative literature both as an undergraduate and a post graduate. He has taught at various academic institutions in the city but most of his time has been given to writing: novels, short stories, literary criticism and reviews. Umberto Eco, Italo Calvino and Jorge Borges are all recognised in the titles of his novels – *The Rose of the Name, Visible Cities* and *Atlas* – which began to appear in the mid-1990s. He has received numerous awards for his writing and spent time teaching creative writing in the United States. In 2017 his collection *Cantonese Love Stories* appeared in the Penguin Hong Kong series.

*Cantonese Love Stories* is a series of twenty-five vignettes of Hong Kong life in the 1990s. The romantic setting of each tale involves lovers thriving or thrashing out a living in the fast-moving, fashion-conscious society that Hong Kong had become. Dung calls them 'sketches' consisting of a loose combination of narrative and description in which the characters are captured at some specific moment or turning point in their lives. While the settings of the stories can be realistic, the sting in the tale is often illusion or, even more so, disillusion as a moment of opportunity passes. Many of Dung's characters are obsessed with fashion accessories.

The first story, 'Agnès b.' is typical of this mix. Ka Tsai has fallen out with his girlfriend the night before and has had an accident leading to his car being taken off the road. Travelling to work by train the next day, he notices a woman with an Agnès b. bag hanging from her left shoulder. She has her back to him but he can see the delicate white of her neck. He also admires her trendy long-sleeved T-shirt and jeans. Although his car is soon repaired Ka Tsai continues to take the train each day looking out for the well-dressed lady. When at last they speak, she tells him that she was a patient of some years back, clearly mistaking him for a doctor who had treated her. Your hands were cold then, she tells him, and swinging her bag, disappears.

In another story two lovers are obsessed with photo stickers which they have taken in a booth especially set up for couples. Kei-Heung has a batch of photos stickers made with Ah Ping, her lover who doesn't believe that they are anything other than images. As time passes, she tires of his seriousness and wants to start a new relationship with another man but Ah Ping will not give her up. Kei-Heung remembers that she has stowed away most of the photo stickers the couple took together. She quickly destroys them. The one remaining photo is the one she gave to Ah Ping which he has stuck on his wallet. The only way she can get it back is to invite him out and while he is visiting the lavatory in the restaurant, finds his wallet and removes and destroys the sticker. When Ah Ping returns to the table, he tells her that after all he thinks they should split up. However, Kei-Heung's new found freedom does not lead to lasting happiness. Her new affair does not last more than a few months; the couple had not taken any photos together in a booth.

Another vignette leads us to Macau and the famous Portuguese custard tarts, the *pasteis de nata*. Pui Pui develops an irresistible taste for the tarts but notices that whenever she eats them, she also has strange dreams. She and her boyfriend, Siu San, both gobble dozens of the tarts each day. On a visit Macau to find the Lord Stow's bakery where they are made, Sui San loses patience with Pui Pui's fantasies and makes for the casino to gamble. Left on her own in the hotel Piu Pui packs her bags to catch the evening ferry back to Hong Kong, telling the curious man next to her the name of the last of the pastries she is eating.

In one story Dung makes fun of the differences between Cantonese and Mandarin. At an elementary evening class for Hong-Kongers wanting to learn Mandarin, a young girl in the back row, Ka Ka, when asked what her favourite colour is by the teacher, says it is khaki pointing to the trousers she is wearing.

'Ah! That is cream colour' says the teacher but Ka Ka says 'no' both in Mandarin and in English. She is watched by Ah Mai, who at first put off by her clumsiness with Mandarin tones, meeting her on the street after class, asks for her phone number. She recites the numbers in broken tones in Mandarin. When they both get soaked in the rain and Ka Ka's trousers are wet, Ah Mai jokes that after all there isn't much difference between khaki and cream. Ka Ka is not amused. When he tries to call her on the number, she has given him, no one at the other end has ever heard of her. Her tones in Mandarin must have distorted the sound of the numbers.

Fashion garments appear in a number of the sketches. A couple who are both basket-ball players adorn themselves with Air Jordan outfits, including sports shoes. At the exhortation of friends, they enter a basket-ball competition with each other. In the competition the boyfriend is beaten by his girlfriend and in his fury at his loss of face, leaves her. In another fashion-based story a brother and sister are united briefly by an Adidas jacket. Skinny, the brother, has left home and Tripper, the sister, wearing the jacket searches for him in the shopping mall where he works in the porn business. He has moved on to another job but she tracks him down. When he unzips his sister's jacket, he sees that she is not wearing anything underneath and runs away ignoring her plea for him to kiss her. She tries to zip up the jacket but the zip is broken.

The obsession with brands shows us that Dung is talking about a modern Hong Kong in which the younger generation behave in a much more liberated way than their parents. A teacher, Miss Choi-sam ('cabbage heart' a nick name used by her students) discovers this when there is an uproar among the girl pupils who notice she is wearing a Gucci watch. She realises that:

*The students were nevertheless quite bright, but excessively diligent and hardworking, so the pressure was heavy. The worst nuisance was that they were more skilful than she was in buying famous brands.*[cxlvi]

Everyone is excited at the arrival of a male teacher, Chan Chi Ching but Miss Choi-sam finds him too serious and dull. However, one day her watch gets stuck on her wrist and struggle though she does, she cannot get it off. In a panic, she rushes round to Chan Chi Ching's apartment and asks him to help her. He manages to release the watch but goes on holding her hand. She asks him to help her again.

In Dung's *Atlas the Archaeology of an Imaginary City* we enter a more abstract way of looking at Hong Kong. In his hands history and fiction are mingled by examining how Hong Kong has been represented in historical maps over the ages. The maps depict an ever-changing set of shifting sites and shapes: the way cartographers have drawn the maps has been determined by their visions of the place, by their understanding of legend and popular aspiration as much as by bricks and stones. Dung tells us:

*The legendary city of Victoria was, like Venus, born from the waves of the sea. It is not known how it disappeared in the end. The legend thus brings us face-to-face with an archaeological question: by what means can we verify a city's existence?* [cxlvii]

Familiar sites and landmarks appear in different places on different maps: sometimes Hong Kong Island is prominent; sometimes it seems to disappear. Its boundaries are also complicated since areas to be reclaimed are marked on some maps; later versions include or exclude such areas depending on the exact time when they are drawn up. Divisions on the maps may not exist in reality: how can the hilly wasteland that was Kowloon be divided into sections? Boundaries drawn on the maps are in fact political, imaginary lines that may have no relation to natural, geographical barriers. Moreover, the science of cartography itself keeps changing: utopias, uni-topias and even imaginary places are drawn in or excluded depending on the cartographer's whims.

An interesting illustration of changes is in the use of the very name, 'Hong Kong'. Dung finds examples of it appearing in seventeenth-century Chinese coastal maps but after that time it disappears to be replaced by the name Hung Heung Lou Shun ('red incense burner guard post'). That name continues to be used until the nineteenth century until 'Hong Kong' is revived by the British to name the island. This suggests that Hong Kong as a place did not exist until Belcher drew up his Hong Kong nautical map after 1841 when the ship *Sulphur* landed at Possession Point on the island's northern shore.

Another early map of Hong Kong was drawn up by the first Governor, Sir Henry Pottinger in 1842. The map is arranged with the south at the top so to read it in the conventional way, it has to be turned upside down. Dung speculates that it was drawn in that way because British interest was directed from the harbour towards the island although he adds that another explanation might be that

Pottinger suffered from inverted vision. One of the purposes of the map was to allocate allotments of land along the shoreline to individuals, such as Jardine of Jardine, Matheson. Prominent public buildings – Government House and the Post Office – are also marked. Although Pottinger's allocated land according to the plan on the map, the Governor overturned the land sales and introduced a different system.

Aldrich Street, also near the shoreline, was another place closely connected to the early Pottinger period. Major Aldrich was one of the signatories to the Treaty of Nanking which ceded Hong Kong Island to the British in 1842 (Kowloon came later in 1860). Aldrich drew up an elaborate scheme in which the main feature of the Central district would be an impregnable fortress dominating and protecting the entire area. His plan was also overruled by Governor Pottinger who insisted that the area should remain primarily commercial rather than assuming a garrison-like character. Aldrich turned his energies to other problems including the disciplining of British troops whose behaviour was rowdy and the protection of locals from pirate raids on their villages. So admired was he for the latter that a temple was dedicated to him. However, it and the bay named after him vanished in modern reclamation in 1999.

Several years after the arrival of the British, in 1845, the Japanese sailor Kino passed through Hong Kong leaving yet another account. At first, he thinks the whole place is deserted as he can see nothing in the thick, morning mist. But then he records:

*As we approached the southern shore of the harbor, the mist was torn apart, there was a great sound of steam whistles, the waves surged, and the ships moved back and forward busily, like suddenly awakened sea creatures. In the swirling fog along the shore, buildings thrust upwards and several thousand residences lined the harborside, row upon row of houses of all shapes and sizes as we drew closer, the seawater seemed to recede from the shoreline, so that an orderly arrangement of streets was revealed, with endless streams of hawkers and fishermen. Everywhere hills had been levelled and large-scale construction was taking place with stone masons, bricklayers, plasterers, carpenters, and coolies numbering in their thousands.* [cxlviii]

This is a thoroughly convincing description of the rapidly emerging city and corresponds to earliest pictorial representations artists have left of it.

The Chinese way of categorising areas made accurate map making even more complicated. It consisted of a distinction between *wan* or ringed areas and *yeuk*, districts within those areas. There were four broad *wan* areas and nine *yeuk*. However, whether the ringed, *wan* areas were chain-shaped relationships or areas that had passed through four stages of change was not clear. *Yeuk* districts were linked to a legend about a tragic love affair in which a young couple failed to meet up nine times. Dung adds laconically that these ambiguities have given rise to a 'debate about Chinese habits and the nature of Chinese cultural traditions'[cxlix] among European cartographers.

Street names provide another set of ambiguities. A striking example is that of Possession Street so named by the British near the point at which Captain Belcher, aboard the *Sulphur*, arrived on the island. In Cantonese the street was named 'mouth of the water course' because it was near a stream coming off the mountain into the sea. In fact, according to *feng shui* divinations the area was regarded as unsuitable for habitation and no one was surprised when it turned into a disreputable, unpleasant district best avoided. On the Kowloon side Mongkok provides an even more exotic puzzle. Formerly an agricultural area with paddy fields, two main streets were named after local produce. Water Spinach Street was so named as the crop grew there in summer but it changed its name to Water Cress Street in winter because that was the crop grown in that season. Eventually, when two streets were created as the area was levelled out and turned into an urban, residential area, the local population moved from one to the other according to the season.

Some anecdotes that Dung relates recreate the atmosphere of an exact historic moment. In 1907 one Mr John Smith arrives aboard the ship *Sunrise* for a single day's visit. He and his wife and friends are carried ashore in a 'bizarre, filthy' sampan 'with the flavour of the Orient'. [cl]After being shown the building of Jardine Matheson, the party adjourn to the Hong Kong Hotel for lunch. In the afternoon while the ladies go to the hairdresser, Smith begins his exploration of Central on foot. He visits the bookshop, Kelly and Walsh (still operation after more than a century) choosing books on Chinese literature and legend to read on his ongoing voyage. He then pops into the chemist shop, Watsons (also still in business), for some medication. In the Afong Studio on Ice House Street, buys some pictures of local people and scenery as souvenirs which he is sure his wife will like. After dinner at the hotel, the group board a sampan once more for their return to *Sunrise*.

Maps dealing with specific scientific matter can also illuminate the city's history. The type of geological underpinning in any area will determine what can be built. In 1986 detailed geological maps were drawn up showing the exact structure of every part of the colony. Much of the urban area of Central and Kowloon were built on sediment with earth dug up for use in reclamation. Rubble and landfill were perfect. Volcanic areas, such as the Peak, were less suitable for building upon.

One of the modern and most telling set of maps to appear are those made for tourists. While previously adverts adorned older maps in boxes on the side, maps entirely dedicated to tourist attractions first appeared in the 1990s. On these maps red circles were used to mark places of recreational or cultural interest: parks, galleries, museums and open-air markets. Green circles marked out cinemas and theatres. Blue circles showed the location of hotels. The tourist map was the latest symbol of the city's self-image as a mecca for visitors. One tourist, staying at Peninsula Hotel records seeing a 'forest of hotels' on the map he has. Then looking at the actual streets he records:

*All the hotel buildings rose from flat ground with nothing in the space between them, so that from a distance it looked like a city of hotels, with only a few so-called scenic spots and historical sites squatting between them.*[cli]

The impression was much the same when the same visitor crossed over to Hong Kong Island and could not see anyone who was not either a tourist or working in a tourist-related job.

Dung's *Atlas* is a complex matrix of styles. He is no longer concerned with fictional characterisation but instead attempts to reconstruct the city's past by examining the maps which have been made of it. But this historical approach is embellished by a highly imaginative element. Although he expounds a contextual theory, it is the element of fantasy that brings his account to life. Fiction is interwoven with history in a highly unusual blend. The climax of this approach is when he considers more exotic examples – digital maps and maps tracing the orbit of time. They confirm Dung's speculation that Victoria is an imaginary city created in various forms by the fancy and hidden intentions of cartographers.

# A Last Word
# Medicine, Music and Archaeology:
# Solomon Bard

This book has been dedicated to how writers have seen Hong Kong and struggled with its identity from the 1950s to 1997. One character whose time in Hong Kong spans this entire period was Solomon Bard, not primarily a writer but medical man, musician and archaeologist. In his memoirs, *Light and Shade*, subtitled *Sketches from an Uncommon Life,* he expresses doubts that his life, eventually lasting nearly a century, would be of special interest to anyone but in fact it spans the entire end of the colonial period, a time of challenges and change in Hong Kong, as we have seen. Bard also compiled a record of Hong Kong history through newspaper coverage in his *Voices from the Past: Hong Kong 1842–1918* (2002) and reported on antiquities in the colony in another book, *In Search of the Past: A Guide to the Antiquities of Hong Kong* (1988).

Solomon was born to a Russian Jewish family who had emigrated to Chita, a small town in Eastern Siberia just before the Bolshevik Revolution of 1917. While much of Russia was in turmoil the family enjoyed a 'Chekhovian' existence in what was a sleepy outpost, with excursions to the countryside for picnics. But the dark clouds gathering persuaded his father that another move was needed so the Bards moved to Harbin in China. Harbin was very much a Russian enclave where other foreigners had also set up businesses. In the Jewish community there was a good school and most importantly for the young Solomon, organised music. Following in his family's artistic footsteps – his grandfather was musical, his uncle a painter – he learned to play the flute and violin as well as the piano and nurtured an ambition for a career as a professional musician.

Harbin boasted a good local orchestra which teenage Solomon joined with great enthusiasm. Voracious reading was his other passion. Before long another move took place – this time to Shanghai where Solomon became a student at the English school, modelled after public schools in England. Finding the discipline stricter than he had been used to and not liking the prefect system, he nevertheless settled into the school and began to enjoy it. He made considerable progress in learning English. When his parents encouraged him to take up a career in medicine, he set his sights on Hong Kong University where the medical school was well-established and had a good, international reputation.

Solomon arrived in Hong Kong in 1934, soon adapting well to his fourth home, with a very different environment from the others. By this time his English was proficient enough for him to pursue a degree without difficulty and before long he was doing the clinical part of the qualification as a medical doctor. His Russian connection could be kept up by contact with refugees in the local community, gathering in favourite spots like Tkachenko patisserie where Russian specialities were served and enjoyed by Joyce Booth, as we have seen. After graduating, Solomon worked in the Hong Kong University Medical Service, eventually being appointed its director in 1956.

But in the meantime, the Japanese invasion of Hong Kong had taken place. Bard had enlisted in the Hong Kong Volunteers so was involved in the fierce battle to defend Hong Kong which ended with surrender on 25th December, 1941. With other military personnel, he was interned during the Japanese Occupation in Sham Shui Po POW Camp in Kowloon for four long years. The camp regime was harsh, with ruthless punishment for even minor offences but the spirit of camaraderie among the prisoners and some collaboration from people outside helped the fittest to survive. After the war and in recognition of his service, Solomon was 'repatriated' to England, a country he ironically records, he had never visited before. With an introduction from Austin, Solomon met Eric Coates, Austin's father in London and presented him with a box of cigars from his son. Solomon greatly admired *Myself a Mandarin* which he calls a 'literary gem'[clii] and he recognised that the lure of the Orient kept Austin from returning to England. But the lure of the East also applied to Solomon: he returned to Hong Kong to take up his medical career once again.

Two post-war activities mark Solomon's time in Hong Kong as remarkable. The first was in his beloved area of music, the second in archaeology. As we have seen Solomon himself arrived in Hong Kong with musical talent developed during his time in Harbin. Not only was he a player of various instruments but he began to develop an interest in conducting. He records that this new-found interest coincided with a feeling of change in the air of liberated, post-war Hong Kong. Cultural activities began to flourish although much needed Government support was slow in coming.

The Sino-British Club was founded, bringing together hitherto fragmented groups of musicians, foreigners and Chinese, under a single baton which in due course fell to Solomon to wield. In 1956 the Orchestra, an offshoot of the Club, was invited by the Canton Arts Festival to visit the city and perform there. Given the political situation at the time, the invitation came as a considerable surprise. Solomon and Tony Braga, another founding member, decided that it would be right to take it up though the local media was hostile, seeing any visit of Hong Kong performers as a propaganda coup for the Communist regime. As it turned out, the orchestra was extremely well received with a traditional, Chinese banquet arranged to honour the guests on arrival. The performances were well attended with enthusiastic audiences. Solomon records that:

*The atmosphere was warm, friendly and relaxed. During the next two days we were shown places of interest around Canton interspersed with sumptuous lunches. Contrary to expectations of our critics in Hong Kong, our hosts behaved correctly at all times and made no political statements or innuendos.*[cliii]

The nascent orchestra metamorphosed into the Hong Kong Philharmonic though its severance from the Sino-British Club upset Tony Braga who resigned from the supervising body. Solomon continued to conduct it through the 1960s, with trips abroad featuring in its schedule. Together with a group of people from the musical and theatrical world, he pursued the need for a permanent venue for the orchestra. In the meantime, concerts were given in a host of halls, cinemas and clubs. A Victorian city hall had been demolished without any replacement before the war so the 'City Hall Campaign' concentrated on the idea of a new one being built and open to the public. To their surprise the Government agreed and eventually, in 1962, the present City Hall opened its doors to the delight of the cultural community in Hong Kong.

Even more remarkable during this period was Solomon Bard's growing interest and commitment to Chinese classical music. To most Westerners who had heard it played only in street processions, Chinese music seemed jangled and discordant. Solomon himself had had no particular exposure to Chinese music in Harbin where the repertoire had been entirely in Western, classical music. Now he started to study it seriously, realising that it had always been an important part of Chinese culture albeit one that had been static for centuries until a new generation of musicians in the twentieth century, influenced by foreign music, began exploring new ways of expression. This included bringing groups of different instruments, hitherto played separately, under a single direction. Solomon explains:

*In many ways a modern Chinese symphony orchestra was an experiment, each orchestra trying to achieve perfect instrumental balance in its own way; there was no standard model, only common features.*[cliv]

He listened to as much Chinese music as he could and to his surprise, was invited as guest-conductor to lead the Hong Kong Chinese Orchestra. From a hesitant beginning, freed from his official duties, he became its principal conductor, leading it to a successful visit to Beijing in 1987. For a Westerner to do this was a remarkable achievement and one, rare example of the assimilation of the two dominant cultures.

Solomon also made a considerable contribution in the field of archaeology. His interest arose while he was still in general practice and later at the University, spurred on by his contact with two academic geologists whom he knew. The dedicated group of supporters, led by the energetic Solomon, would walk around the Hong Kong hills and dales on weekends, surveying the rock formations. One of its most spectacular finds was of ancient stone tools indicating that the Hong Kong islands had been inhabited in the Stone Age. In due course the group uncovered many Neolithic sites in the New Territories and on some of the islands including ones on Lantau.

Eventually the University Archaeological Team was wound up and the Hong Kong Archaeological Society was founded, an institution which aimed at stirring up public interest as well as guarding local sites of interest. Solomon was keen on persuading the Government to protect the colony's varied historical heritage. In 1972 a significant step was taken when the Antiquities Advisory Office was set up. By that time Solomon had retired from the University and happily took up the role of principal executive, thereby entering the Hong Kong civil service. The remit of the Office was wide: it included the protection of historic buildings (whether of Chinese or European style), archaeological sites, traditional Chinese villages (with their ancient boundaries), ancient engravings wherever they might be and the temples and forts scattered across the colony.

To increase his own knowledge Solomon sought an attachment to the Department of the Environment (later English Heritage) in the United Kingdom to learn among other things how to organise the new body. That lasted about a month and he found the experience extremely useful. When he returned to Hong Kong, he took the decision to concentrate on one major repair and restoration project. His choice fell on the old ruined Chinese fort on Tung Lung Island, at the eastern approaches to Hong Kong harbour. The existence of the fort had been known for some time but it was marked as a ruin on the official ordinance map. Over a period of several years, with the help of a group of volunteers known as the 'Tung Lung Ladies', painstaking fieldwork was undertaken which included removing large amounts of rubble and damaged bricks from collapsed walls. Typically, Solomon also involved the local population of peasant farmers, persuading them that the project enhanced the reputation of their island. They became invaluable, hard-working volunteers. Eventually the fort was restored to a safe standard and has since been on the tourist route in Hong Kong.

Solomon Bard's contributions to Hong Kong life were remarkable. In his early life as something of an outsider in Siberia and then in China, he became an insider in Hong Kong playing a significant part in its cultural life. His passion led him to cross cultural barriers which, as we have seen in the stories of so many of the writers of the period, was unusual except among individuals who braved sometimes harsh criticism for daring to defy social conventions. Those individuals, including Solomon, are the heroes of *My Hong Kong*.

# Bibliography

Bard, Solomon. *In Search of the Past. A guide to the Antiquities of Hong Kong.*

Hong Kong: Hong Kong Urban Council, 1988.

---- *Light and Shade. Sketches from an Uncommon Life.*

Hong Kong: Hong Kong University Press, 2009.

*Voices from the Past. Hong Kong 1842–1918.*

Hong Kong: Hong Kong University Press, 2002.

Blunden, Edmund. *A Hong Kong House. Poems 1951–1961*. London: Collins, 1962.

Booth, Martin. *Gweilo Memories of a Hong Kong Childhood.* London : Doubleday, 2004.

Chi-Kwan, Mark. *'Development with Decolonisation? Hong Kong's Future*

*Relations with Britain and China, 1967–1972.'*

Cambridge: Journal of Royal Asiatic Society, Vol 24 Part 2 April, 2014.

*City Voices. Hong Kong Writing in English 1945 to the Present*

eds. Xu Xi and Mike Ingham. Hong Kong: Hong Kong University Press, 2003.

Coates, Austin. *City of Broken Promises*. Hong Kong: Hong Kong University Press, 2009.

----*Myself A Mandarin*. London: Frederick Muller, 1968.

----*The Road.* London
: Hutchinson, 1959.

Dung Kai-cheung. *Atlas. The Archaeology of an Imaginary City*. New York: Columbia University Press, 2007.

*Cantonese Love Stories. Twenty-Five Vignettes of a City.*

Australia: Penguin Publishing, 2007.

Elegant, Simon. *A Chinese Wedding.* London: Piatkus, 1998.

Feng Chi-shun. *Diamond Hill. Memories of growing up in a Hong Kong Squatter village.* Hong Kong: Blacksmith Books, 2009.

Greenway, Alice. *White Ghost Girls.* London
: Atlantic Books,2006.

Ho, Elaine Yee Lin, *Contexts and Intertexts*. Manchester: Manchester University Press, 2000.

Ingham, Michael. *Hong Kong A Cultural and Literary History.* Oxford: Signal Books, 2007.

Lanchester, John. *Fragrant Harbour*. London
: Faber, 2002.

Lin Tai-yi Kampoon *Street.* Cleveland and New York: World, 1964.

Lee, Janice Y. K. *The Expatriates*. London
: Little Brown Book Group, 2016.

---- *The Piano Teacher.* London: Harper Press, 2009.

Leighton, Iain. *Footprints Left in Hong Kong Expat Life in Hong Kong in the 1950s and 1960s.* UK: Amazon, 2020.

---- *A Hong Kong Time Capsule My Childhood in Hong Kong in the 1950s.* Italy: Amazon, 2021.

Mason, Richard. *The World of Suzie Wong.* London : Signet Books, 1968.

Mo, Timothy. *An Insular Possession.* New York: Random House, 1986.

----*The Monkey King.* London: Paddleless, 2000.

---- *Sour Sweet.* London : Andre Deutsch, 1982.

Suyin, Han. *A Many-Splendoured Thing.* London: Jonathan Cape, 1952.

---- *My House has Two Doors.* London: Triad Grafton, 1988.

Theroux, Paul. *Kowloon Tong.* Boston & New York: Houghton Mifflin Company 1997.

Xu Xi. *Dear Hong Kong.* London: Penguin, 2017.

---- *Hong Kong Rose.* Hong Kong: Chameleon Press, 2004.

---- *Unwalled City A Novel of Hong Kong.* Hong Kong: Chameleon Press, 2007. Wong, David T. K.

*Collected Hong Kong Stories.* Hong Kong: Blacksmith, 2016.

----*Hong Kong Short Stories.* Hong Kong: Blacksmith, 2016.

----*The Evergreen Tea House a Hong Kong Novel.* Hong Kong: Muse, 2003.

# Notes

---

## Chapter 1

[i] Austin Coates, *Myself A Mandarin* (London, 1968) p. 1.

[ii] Ibid. p. 107.

[iii] Ibid. p. 7.

[iv] Ibid. p. 175.

[v] Ibid. p. 92.

[vi] Ibid. p. 226.

[vii] Ibid. p. 22.

[viii] Austin Coates, *The Road* (London, 1959) p. 13.

[ix] Ibid. p. 43.

[x] Ibid. p. 82.

[xi] Austin Coates, *City of Broken Promises*, (Hong Kong, 2009) p. 285.

[xii] Ibid. p. 254.

[xiii] Ibid. p. 175.

[xiv] Ibid. p. 110.

## Chapter 2

[xv] Han Suyin, *A Many-Splendoured Thing* (London, 1952) p. 66.

[xvi] Ibid. p. 74.

[xvii] Ibid. p. 257.

[xviii] Ibid. p. 21.

[xix] Ibid. p. 285.

[xx] Han Suyin, *My House has Two Doors* (London, 1988) p. 63.

xxi Ibid.

xxii Han Suyin, *A Many-Splendoured Thing* p. 81.

xxiii Han Suyin, *My House has Two Doors* p. 14.

xxiv Ibid. p. 14.

xxv Han Suyin, *A Many-Splendoured* Thing p. 111.

xxvi Ibid. p. 183.

xxvii Ibid. p. 195.

xxviii Ibid. p. 120.

xxix Ibid. p. 201.

## Chapter 3

xxx Martin Booth, *Gweilo Memories of a Hong Kong Childhood* (London, 2004) p. 3.

xxxi Ibid. p. 65.

xxxii Ibid. p. 53.

xxxiii Ibid. p. 104.

xxxiv Ibid. p. 244.

xxxv Ibid. p. 103.

xxxvi Ibid. p. 323.

xxxvii Ibid. p. 202.

xxxviii Ibid. p. 213.

xxxix Ibid. p. 236.

xl Ibid. p. 238.

xli Ibid. p. 119.

xlii Ibid. p. 258.

xliii Ibid. p. 265.

xliv Ibid.

## Chapter 4

xlv Feng Chi-shun, *Diamond Hill* (Hong Kong, 2009) p. 8.

xlvi Ibid. p. 122.

xlvii Ibid. p. 119.

xlviii Ibid. P. 117.

[xlix] Ibid. p. 146.
[l] Ibid. p. 156.
[li] Ibid. p. 133.

## Chapter 5

[lii] Richard Mason, *The World of Suzie Wong* (London, 1957) p. 30.
[liii] Ibid. p. 110.
[liv] Ibid. p. 158.
[lv] Ibid. p. 167.
[lvi] Ibid. p. 265.
[lvii] Ibid. p. 168.
[lviii] Ibid. p. 208.
[lix] Ibid. p. 226.

## Chapter 6

[lx] Jean Amato, *Asian American Novelists: A Biographical Critical Source Book* (Connecticut, 2000) p. 361.
[lxi] Lin Tai-yi, *Kampoon Street* (Cleveland, 1964) p. 52.
[lxii] Ibid. p. 83.
[lxiii] Ibid. p. 87.
[lxiv] Ibid. p. 100.
[lxv] Ibid. p. 119/120.
[lxvi] Ibid. p. 201.
[lxvii] Ibid. p. 13.
[lxviii] Ibid. p. 248.

## Chapter 7

[lxix] Timothy Mo, *The Monkey King* (London, 2000) p. 18.
[lxx] Ibid. p. 79.
[lxxi] Ibid. p. 51.
[lxxii] Ibid. p. 254.
[lxxiii] Timothy Mo, *Sour Sweet* (London, 1982) p. 1.
[lxxiv] Ibid. p. 2.

[lxxv] Ibid. p. 137.
[lxxvi] Ibid. p. 21.
[lxxvii] Ibid. p. 24.

## Chapter 8

[lxxviii] Janice Y K Lee, *The Piano Teacher* (London, 2009) Conversation, p. 2
[lxxix] Ibid. p. 1.
[lxxx] Janice T K Lee, op.cit., p. 4.
[lxxxi] Ibid. p. 42.
[lxxxii] Ibid. p. 185.
[lxxxiii] Ibid. p. 262.
[lxxxiv] Janice Y K Lee *the Expatriates* (London, 2016) p. 86.
[lxxxv] Ibid. p. 95/96.
[lxxxvi] Ibid. p. 88.
[lxxxvii] Ibid. p. 73.

## Chapter 9

[lxxxviii] Alice Greenway, *The White Ghost Girls* (London, 2006) p. 1.
[lxxxix] Ibid. p. 14.
[xc] Ibid. p. 17.
[xci] Ibid. p 39/40.
[xcii] Ibid. p. 39.
[xciii] Ibid. p. 173.

## Chapter 10

[xciv] Christopher New, *The Chinese Box* (Hong Kong, 2001) p. 18.
[xcv] Ibid. p. 28.
[xcvi] Ibid. p. 68.
[xcvii] Ibid. p. 30.
[xcviii] Christopher New, *A Change of Flag* (Hong Kong, 2000) p. 71.
[xcix] Ibid. p. 263.
[c] Ibid. p. 107.
[ci] Ibid. p. 27.
[cii] Ibid. p. 188.

## Chapter 11

[ciii] Xu Xi, *Hong Kong Rose* (Hong Kong, 2004) p. 37.
[civ] Ibid. p. 263.
[cv] Ibid. p. 190.
[cvi] Ibid. p. 227/228.
[cvii] Xu Xi, *The Unwalled City* (Hong Kong, 2001) p. 307.
[cviii] Ibid. p. 104.
[cix] Ibid. p. 280.
[cx] Xu Xi, *Dear Hong Kong* (Australia, 2017) p. 1.
[cxi] Ibid. p. 90.
[cxii] Xu Xi, 'Why I Stopped Being Chinese' (The Iowa Review, Vol 45 Issue 1, 2015) p. 39.
[cxiii] Ibid., p. 40.
[cxiv] Xu Xi, *Dear Hong Kong*, p. 93.

## Chapter 12

[cxv] John Lanchester, *Fragrant Harbour* (London, 2002) p. 91.
[cxvi] Ibid. p. 91.
[cxvii] Ibid. p. 92.
[cxviii] Ibid. p. 92

## Chapter 13

[cxix] Simon Elegant, *A Chinese Wedding* (London, 1994) p. 3.
[cxx] Ibid. p. 119.
[cxxi] Ibid. p. 44.
[cxxii] Ibid. p. 161/2.

## Chapter 14

[cxxiii] Paul Theroux, *Kowloon Tong* (New York, 1997) p. 52.
[cxxiv] Ibid. p. 112.
[cxxv] Ibid. p. 156.
[cxxvi] Ibid. p. 184.
[cxxvii] Ibid. p. 243.

[cxxviii] Fionnvala McHugh, 'Stranger than Fiction' (South China Morning Post, 29 November, 2014)

[cxxix] Paul Theroux , *Kowloon Tong* p. 76.

[cxxx] Anthony Grant 'All Change is Fascinating' (Atlantic Unbound Interviews, July 3rd 1997).

[cxxxi] Fionnvala McHugh, 'Stranger Than Fiction.'

[cxxxii] Anthony Grant, 'All Change is Fascinating.'

[cxxxiii] Kevin Kwong quoted in Fionnvala McHugh, 'Stranger than Fiction.'

## Chapter 15

[cxxxiv] David T K Wong, *Collected Hong Kong Stories* (Hong Kong, 2018) p. 9.

[cxxxv] Ibid. p. 109.

[cxxxvi] Ibid. p. 122.

[cxxxvii] Ibid. p. 133.

[cxxxviii] Ibid. p. 204.

[cxxxix] David T K Wong, *The Evergreen Tea House* (Hong Kong, 2003) p. 83

[cxl] Ibid. p. 47.

[cxli] Ibid. p. 147.

[cxlii] Ibid. p. 149.

[cxliii] Ibid. p. 57.

[cxliv] Ibid. p. 126.

[cxlv] Ibid. p. 160

## Chapter 16

[cxlvi] Dung Kai-Cheung, *Cantonese Love Stories* (Australia, 2017) p. 78.

[cxlvii] Dung Kai-Cheung, *Atlas the Archaeology of an Imaginary City* (New York, 2011) p. 45.

[cxlviii] Ibid. p. 49.

[cxlix] Ibid. p. 58.

[cl] Ibid. p. 64.

[cli] Ibid. p. 146.

**A Last Word**

[clii] Solomon Bard, *Light and Shade Sketches from an Uncommon Life* (Hong Kong, 2009) p. 157.
[cliii] Ibid. p. 149.
[cliv] Ibid. p. 246.

# Index

Aberdeen ................................................................ 22, 40, 42, 95, 120

Africa ................................................................................ 1, 71, 148

Ah Lan ...................................................................... 3, 7, 13, 16, 47

Aldrich, Major ................................................................................ 173

Algiers, ................................................................................................ 47

Anastasia, Princess ............................................................................ 50

Antiquities Advisory Office .............................................................. 179

Auden, W. H. ............................................................................ 71, 140

Australia .................................................................... 105, 158, 182


Bank of China .............................................................................. 49, 57

Bard, Solomon ........................................ 176, 177, 178, 180, 181

Beijing ............................................................ 120, 156, 157, 179

Bela Vista Hotel (Macau) ................................................................ 153

Blunden, Edmund .................................................................... 8, 181

Bolsheviks ............................................................................................ 50

Bombay .......................................................................................... 47, 71

Booth, Joyce .............................................................. 34, 67, 177

Booth, Martin ................... 37, 39, 46, 60, 65, 66, 101, 108, 111, 130, 168, 181

Borges, Jorge .................................................................................... 169

Botanical Gardens ................................................................................ 39

Braga, Tony ...................................................................................... 178

Britain ..................... 11, 99, 105, 120, 134, 143, 148, 157, 181

British Empire ........................................................................ 116, 134

Brussels ................................................................................................ 32

Buddhist ........................................ 22, 23, 69, 89, 114, 164

Burma ............................................................................................ 17, 71

C'hing Ming Festival..................................................................................... 14, 90
Calvino, Italo ............................................................................................... 169
Canton........................................................................... 28, 102, 111, 158, 178
Canton Arts Festival ..................................................................................... 178
Cantonese                    1, 7, 13, 14, 22, 23, 25, 26, 29, 35, 36, 47, 48, 51, 61
                            62, 65, 66, 67, 72, 76, 88, 89, 90, 95, 96, 97, 99, 103
                            107, 114, 116, 119, 125, 128, 132, 133, 136, 138
                            142, 143, 144, 146, 147, 155, 163, 166, 169, 170, 174, 182
Catholic Church............................................................................................. 69
Central ......................13, 49, 57, 74, 83, 104, 119, 125, 132, 154, 173, 174, 175
Cheung Chou ................................................................................................ 111
Chi Lin Monastery.......................................................................................... 68
China                       11, 17, 18, 19, 23, 25, 28, 29, 32, 33, 34, 35, 36, 37, 39, 42
                            43, 44, 48, 49, 51, 52, 56, 59, 60, 61, 70, 77, 79, 80, 102, 104, 106
                            110, 111, 112, 113, 116, 117, 118, 119, 120, 121, 122, 123, 124
                            125, 131, 133, 134, 135, 136, 138, 139, 141, 142, 143, 145, 147
                            149, 150, 153, 156, 157, 158, 159, 160, 163, 164, 167, 169, 176, 180, 181
Chinese New Year....................................................... 40, 56, 95, 112, 122
Chinese university of Hong Kong ................................................................ 126
Ching dynasty ............................................................................... 19, 51, 52
Chiu Chow..................................................................................................... 61
Chou en Lai ................................................................................................... 37
Chung King ............................................................................................. 32, 43
City Hall ...................................................................................................... 178
Coates, Austin.            7, 17, 32, 33, 34, 38, 45, 49, 52, 71, 76, 88, 89
                            92, 93, 97, 99, 101, 104, 108, 110, 127, 130
                            133, 155, 156, 168, 177, 182, 192
Columbia University....................................................................... 79, 182
Communist                  11, 18, 19, 33, 36, 37, 38, 43, 44, 47, 58, 60
                            80, 116, 120, 142, 164, 167, 178
Confucianism.......................................................................... 36, 42, 43
Confucius............................................................................... 79, 164
Connaught Street ........................................................................ 102
Corfu (Ship)................................................................................. 46
Crown Collection.................................................................... 105, 106
Cultural Revolution ........................... 11, 36, 110, 116, 121, 125, 141, 142, 161

Dairy Farm......................................................................................... 52
Deep Water Bay.................................................................................. 40
Des Voeux Road, Central ............................................................ 57, 119
Diamond Hill .......................... 60, 61, 64, 65, 66, 67, 69, 70, 169, 182
Diocesan College................................................................................ 60
Downs Malvern School .................................................................... 71
Dung Kai-Cheung............................................................................ 169

East, the ...................................................... 8, 28, 79, 116, 139, 177
Eco, Umberto.................................................................................... 169
Elegant, Simon................................................................................ 143, 182
English                     1, 13, 19, 20, 22, 24, 29, 30, 32, 34, 35, 36, 42, 43
                          50, 59, 63, 66, 67, 69, 72, 88, 89, 95, 96, 97, 98, 99
                          101, 102, 103, 104, 105, 113, 116, 120, 122, 126, 127
                          132, 133, 135, 136, 148, 150, 162, 171, 177, 180, 181
Eurasian                  11, 32, 34, 37, 43, 45, 60, 72, 77, 104, 105
                          109, 121, 127, 130, 131, 132, 133, 143, 162, 168

Fan Ling............................................................................................. 52
Feng Chi-shun ......................................................... 60, 64, 169, 182
Foreign Correspondents' Club........................................................ 147
Four Seasons Hotel ..................................................... 47, 51, 57
Fragrant Harbour ....................................................... 138, 143, 157, 182

Gable, Clark.............................................................................. 55, 67
Garden Road...................................................................... 15, 54, 95
Gloucester Hotel ........................................................................ 38, 74
Governor's Walk ............................................................................... 54
Grantham, Sir Alexander (Governor)....................................37, 46, 58
Greenway, Alice ..................................... 110, 116, 122, 127, 142, 182
Gweilos................................................................ 15, 92, 127, 132, 157

Han Suyin                 32, 33, 34, 35, 36, 37, 38, 39, 40, 41, 42
                          43, 44, 45, 58, 61, 67, 76, 79, 80
                          101, 104, 125, 127, 133, 143, 192
Happy Valley......................................... .....34,37,57,77,104,150,151

Harbin .................................................................. 117, 176, 177, 178
Hei Ling Chou ............................................................................ 53
Helena May Institute .................................................................. 54
Henan province............................................................................ 32
Ho Man Tin .................................................................... 51, 68, 92
Holden, William .......................................................................... 67
Hong Kong and Shanghai Bank ................................................. 57
Hong Kong Arts Festival ............................................................ 18
Hong Kong Chinese Orchestra ................................................. 179
Hong Kong Club............................................... 95, 139, 150, 154
Hong Kong Government ................................... 17, 18, 35, 79
Hong Kong Hotel............................................................... 38, 174
Hong Kong University...................... 60, 113, 116, 169, 177, 181, 182
Hong Kong Volunteers .............................................................. 177
Hunter College........................................................................... 101

Ice House Street......................................................................... 174

Jack, Malcolm............................................................................ 1, 13
Japan, Japanese............................................... 25, 71, 93, 104, 148
Japanese invasion ............................................... 54, 102, 105, 177
Jardine Matheson................................................... 39, 113, 174
Jockey Club ...................................................................... 103, 139
Jones, Jennifer ............................................................................ 67

Kai Tak (Airport)............................................... 28, 43, 105, 113
Kang Hsi (Emperor) .................................................................... 99
Kelly and Walsh (Bookstore) ................................................... 174
Kennedy Road ............................................................................. 15
King George V (KGV School) ............................................. 63, 92
Korean ......................................................................... 11, 101, 107
Korean war ............................................................................ 32, 54
Kowloon                    11, 12, 14, 15, 19, 34, 39, 47, 48, 49, 50, 51
                           52, 53, 56, 57, 60, 62, 68, 75, 95, 102, 104, 105
                           112, 113, 120, 138, 139, 140, 141, 147, 154
                           169, 172, 173, 174, 175, 177
Kowloon Motor Bus ..................................................................... 62

Kowloon Tong .......................................... 41, 130, 135, 148, 149, 154, 155, 183

Kuala Lumpur ............................................................................................... 17

La Salle (School) ........................................................................ 60, 63, 169

Lan Kwai Fong ........................................................................ 125, 130, 133, 134

Lanchester, John ............................................................................. 138, 182

Lane Crawford (Department Store) ............................................... 102, 130

Lantau ................................................ 18, 26, 28, 30, 52, 107, 153, 179

Lao-Tze ......................................................................................................... 79

Lee, Janice ................. 26, 101, 102, 104, 106, 107, 109, 119, 130, 140, 157, 182

Li Po ............................................................................................. 42, 143

Lin Tai-Yi ............................................................................. 79, 80, 86, 182

Lisboa Hotel (Macau) .................................................................... 153

Little Red Book ............................................................................. 11, 118

London                                      .... 6, 28, 32, 96, 118, 119, 138, 149
                                        152, 153, 159, 160, 177, 181, 182, 183, 192

Long March, the ......................................................................................... 110

Los Angeles Times ............................................................................. 149

Luk Kwok Hotel ............................................................................. 72

Macau ................18, 28, 29, 30, 41, 45, 50, 75, 89, 106, 120, 150, 151, 153, 170

MacDonnell Road ............................................................................. 15

Malaya ......................................................................................................... 33

Man Lo Temple ............................................................................. 55

Manchu ......................................................................................................... 21

Mandarin                        17, 18, 24, 25, 33, 61, 66, 68, 113, 123, 130, 133
                                        134, 135, 136, 142, 170, 171, 177, 182, 192

Mao Tse Tung ............................................... 13, 15, 110, 118, 161, 164, 165

Maryknoll Convent ............................................................................. 13, 126

Mason, Richard ............................................... 67, 71, 72, 75, 76, 173, 183

Massachusetts ............................................................................. 148

May Road ............................................................................. 15, 55, 77, 102, 104

Ming (Dynasty and Objects) ............................. 48, 52, 56, 79, 89, 99, 164

Mo, Timothy ............................................................................. 32, 49, 88, 133, 183

Mongkok ............................................................................. 56, 80, 96, 174

Moon Festival ............................................................................. 40

Mount Austin ............................................................................. 53, 54, 57, 58

Naipul, V. S. ................................................... 148, 155
Nanking, Treaty of.................................................. 173
Nathan Road, ............................................ 48, 95, 130, 138
Nationalist............................................................ 18, 32
Neolithic sites ........................................................... 179
New Territories....                17, 19, 20, 24, 33, 52, 76, 82, 86, 88, 92
                                                96, 118, 130, 140, 179
New York ...................... 74, 101, 126, 127, 128, 129, 133, 138, 143, 182, 183
New, Christopher........................................... 116, 129, 167
Nina ............................................................. 7, 13, 14, 15, 16
North Point ........................................................ 68, 124

Opium War ..................................................... 52, 89, 157
Oxford............................................................. 88, 138, 182

P & O............................................................... 102, 139
Peak School ............................................................... 54
Peak Tram.................................. 53, 54, 55, 58, 77, 95, 139
Peak, the ........................................... 34, 124, 139, 154
Pearl River .............................................................. 153
Peking ........................................... 25, 34, 118, 165
Penang ................................................................... 17
Peninsula Hotel............................................ 58, 95, 102, 175
Pokfulam.................................... 38, 41, 54, 111, 120
Polynesia................................................................ 71
Portuguese ................................... 29, 30, 63, 104, 170
Pottinger Street .................................................. 102, 173
Pottinger, Sir Henry (Governor)............................ 172, 173
Praia Grande (Macau)............................................ 41, 120

Queen Mary Hospital.......................................... 32, 41, 162

Red army ................................................... 18, 120, 165
Red Guards ............................... 110, 111, 112, 113, 118
Repulse Bay................................. 40, 83, 84, 86, 92, 120
Repulse Bay Hotel.................................................... 92
Revolution 1949 .............................................. 19, 120

Robinson Road ................................................................ 89, 90, 92

Rodamillans, Roman ........................................................... 76

Rome.................................................................................. 71

Royal Airforce .................................................................... 71


Sarawak ............................................................................. 17

Sha Tin............................................................................... 52

Sham Shui Po POW Camp ............................................... 177

Shanghai, Shanghainese           33, 34, 35, 36, 57, 61, 63, 67, 72, 80, 91
                    103, 113, 116, 117, 119, 125, 127, 132, 140, 141, 177

Shau Kei Wan..................................................................... 57

Shek Kip Mei (Squatter Camp) ......................................... 60

Sichuan ....................................................................... 65, 110

Singapore ............................... 33, 47, 134, 148, 150, 157, 158

Sino-British Club.............................................................. 178

Soho (Hong Kong)...................................................... 97, 161

Stanley Prison Camp ........................................................ 106

Star Ferry ....................... 15, 58, 83, 84, 86, 95, 120, 138

Sumatra............................................................................. 42

Tai Lam Cheung ............................................................... 102

Tang era........................................................................... 140

Taoism .......................................................................... 43, 79

Theroux, Paul ................... 41, 130, 148, 149, 154, 155, 156, 157, 183

Tibet................................................................................. 110

Tkachenko...............................................................58, 103, 177


Triad ......................... 62, 64, 69, 98, 99, 100, 124, 141, 183

Tsim Sha Shui................................................................... 135

Tung Lung Island............................................................. 180


Uganda.............................................................................. 148

United States..... 60, 101, 108, 110, 126, 136, 143, 144, 145
                                      146, 158, 161, 166, 169

University Archaeological Team....................................... 179


Vietnam ........................................................................... 110


Wall Street Journal ......................................................... 143

Walled City ........................................................................ 51, 65, 66

Wanchai ............................... 57, 72, 77, 80, 95, 96, 123, 125, 146, 154

Washington Post ...................................................................... 110

Water Spinach Street ................................................................ 174

Waterloo Road ............................................................... 47, 51, 62

Wong, David T K ...................................................................... 158

Xu Xi ...................... 125, 126, 127, 130, 134, 135, 136, 155, 181, 183

Yale ......................................................................................... 79

Yau Ma Tei ......................................................... 14, 47, 49, 56, 80

Yenching university .................................................................. 32